DAD'S SUCCESS

Alfredo Metoyer

AF421865

ISBN 979-8-89112-509-4 (Paperback)
ISBN 979-8-89112-074-7 (Hardcover)
ISBN 979-8-89112-073-0 (Digital)

Copyright © 2024 Alfredo Metoyer
All rights reserved
First Edition

All rights reserved. No part of this publication may be reproduced, distributed, or transmitted in any form or by any means, including photocopying, recording, or other electronic or mechanical methods without the prior written permission of the publisher. For permission requests, solicit the publisher via the address below.

Covenant Books
11661 Hwy 707
Murrells Inlet, SC 29576
www.covenantbooks.com

This book is affectionately dedicated to my son, Jarrad Wayne, whom I love and never wanted to ever think of his dad as a failure. Though I've had my share of troubles, hardships, difficulties, struggles, and worst of all, sins he has seen in me, I want him to always know that my confidence, trust, and commitment will always be in Jesus Christ.

Contents

Chapter 1

It was a very dry summer. It did not rain all season until the minister had begun concluding his eulogy for Juan Felipé DeLeon. The rain did not pour; it just steadily drizzled and appeared like mist for the duration of the day. Attendees of the funeral wept as they departed, and it seemed that heaven was weeping also. The Earth had lost the benefit of another good life.

Among the hundred or so people that were gathered, only one seemed to be unaffected. In fact, he had a look that showed relief that the whole event was over. This was Juan Felipé's son, Carlos. He stood next to the grave with his wife Evelyn and his mother Lucita on each side of him. Certain people were coming to them before leaving and encouraging Lucita and shaking Carlos' hand, telling him his father was a fine man. Carlos didn't think so! After shaking a few hands, he just turned to Evelyn and told her he was getting the car, and quickly, he left.

Carlos was angry with his father, and this anger had lasted more than fifteen years. In all that time, the two had not spoken to each other. The only time the two had been seen together during that time was when he had married his beautiful and wealthy wife, Evelyn. They only met to pose for wedding portraits and then parted from one another.

Carlos approached his vehicle, a shiny and new Cadillac CT5-V Blackwing with an all-wheel drive. He reached for the remote in his jacket pocket and unlocked the door and started the engine with the press of two buttons. Getting inside the car and settling into his seat, he stared off at the remaining few gathered at the gravesite with Evelyn and Lucita. He immediately started to reflect about his father.

Juan Felipé was not a great man by any means, at least in Carlos' estimation. Juan Felipé never graduated high school; in fact, he barely made it through the ninth grade. He never even held a steady job. He would work, as it was available to him. Sometimes he would work at the paper factory, and at other times, he would work in the cannery. In between these jobs, when he was laid off, he would deliver newspapers and collect cans, which he would turn in for their recyclable value. No matter what would happen to him, you would always find Juan Felipé keeping himself busy and gainfully employed. This was a belief that he would always tell his son: "A man was worthless if he did not work!"

Carlos remembered that saying well and caught himself just sitting there, staring. He looked around the interior of the cabin of his vehicle and thought to himself how his diligence and luck had brought him far beyond his dad's standard of living. He had done pretty well for himself, he thought! He engaged the gearshift and brought the car up curbside to the area of the gravesite, honked, then waited.

Pastor Angelo stood alone with Lucita, still talking with her as Evelyn waited aside. Lucita was crying, but she was shaking her head in agreement to whatever it was that Pastor Angelo had been telling her. He turned Lucita toward the car and put his arms around each of the women as he walked them to the car. After opening the doors and seating the women, he walked about the car to address Carlos before they left.

"Hi, Carlos, my sermons will never be the same again!"

"Hello, Pastor Angelo. What do you mean your sermons will never be the same again?"

"Your father started attending my church about fifteen years ago. He was always a quiet man, except when he would pray. It always gave me confidence to preach, knowing that I had someone who would pray for me before, during, and after my sermons. I attribute part of the success of my ministry, for the past decade and a half, to his service. You ought to be proud of him!"

"Pastor, I have not spoken to my father in fifteen years, and now it appears I won't. Am I proud of him? Well, he was my father, and that's that!"

"Carlos, perhaps you should come by and talk with me privately about this. You and Evelyn are more than welcome at our home and church…"

"No! Evelyn and I are fine, and we thank you for sharing." At this, he drove away.

Evelyn was quite embarrassed by the exchange, and as soft spoken as she was, she felt compelled to say something, "Did you have to be so rude to Pastor Angelo? He wasn't trying to make you angry. He sounds like he really misses your dad."

"Evelyn, I appreciate your concern, dear, but everyone misses my dad. You know why? Because everyone has used my dad for one reason or another. All he believed was that a man should work, work, and work. People took advantage of ol' Juan Felipé. 'Do this for me,' 'do that for me,' rarely ever paying him. He was too kind and people took advantage. I've seen a lot of people, even in our own company that are in the same social class as my dad. They have a decent home, car, and lifestyle, but not my dad. He was raised poor, lived poor, and stayed poor."

Evelyn started to squirm and brace for shock. "Carlos, keep your eyes on the road and slow down. You don't have to get all worked up over what the pastor said to you!"

Carlos looked ahead and saw that he was veering over the centerline on the road and about to collide into an oncoming vehicle. He maneuvered right back into his lane. Evelyn tightened her seatbelt and glanced a stare at him. Carlos slowed his speed and began talking again, as if he did not want to lose his train of thought. He cleared his throat and continued speaking.

"Evelyn, my dad was a good man, perhaps too good for his own good. He never hesitated to help anybody, sometimes at his family's expense. I mean…he was there for us, but his good for other people never helped us out. He taught me to work hard, and for that I'm thankful, but in everything he had done, he doesn't have any success to show for it. I grew up always seeing this, and I thought the only way that I would have a better life is to go to college. This is where he let me down. He could bend over backward to help someone else, but he wouldn't cosign a loan for my education. He said he never wanted to be in debt and suggested that I get a job and save the money for school. When he told me that, I figured I would never be able to go. That was when I decided to enlist in the military to get the benefit of the GI Bill for school, plus it would move me out of the house." Evelyn appeared perplexed at the outburst and sudden revelation of her husband's relationship with his father. She had no idea that this frustration had been so well kept inside of Carlos. She never expected such an attitude out of him because he was always so upbeat and positive, self-controlled, and cool-headed.

Glancing back at Mama Lucita, Evelyn tried to lighten the mood and said, "Carlos, but he was proud of you, and—"

"Evelyn," Carlos interrupted, "didn't you hear me? My dad and I have not talked to each other for fifteen years. Never once did he tell *me* he was proud of *me*! There sure would have been plenty of opportunities for him to say something to *me* to show his pride. He never said anything to *me*!"

"Not a word?" Evelyn asked. "Not even a letter?" The reality of the fact started to sink into her.

"Honey, I sure wish he would have. He could have told me he was proud of me completing boot camp, or he could have said something when I came back alive after invading Iraq. He could have said he was proud when I was accepted at the university, or when I had to still work and carry a full course load of study and still graduate with honors. How about showing his pride when I got my job and helped it to be a Fortune 100 company? He never even said a word of congratulations to me for finding you. I would call and write Mama, and he would never say a word or drop a note with Mama's…"

Just then, you can hear Lucita's crying in the backseat as she covered her face and began to mutter to herself repeatedly, "Ohhh, what am I going to do?"

Carlos approached the modest rental that he had grown up in and slowed to a stop. Carlos had thought that his mother had start worrying about life without his dad, so he turned around and began to explain his intentions.

"Mama, Evelyn and I discussed your being alone now, and we agree that you should live with us now. Now why don't you gather some things and come and stay with us. We have plenty of room for you. We will take care of you. Okay, Mama?"

Lucita wiped her tears and began to speak. It was difficult because she was controlling her anger, but as she continued, her voice intensified, and she said, "Carlos, I have never once yelled at you, and I regret that this is the day. You are so much like your father, stubborn as a mule! Today we have buried him, and all you can do is talk about how mad you are at him. Are you ashamed of him, Carlos? He didn't need your shame. He was ashamed of himself!"

Carlos tried to speak. "Mama, come on. I'll help you gather some things."

"No! Now listen to me!" Lucita yelled. "I am not going anywhere. I am fine with living alone. I have enough to live on, and the church always will look after me. I want to tell *you* something that your father didn't want *you* to know. I think it's good I tell you.

"Carlos, your father lived by the old ways of his people. When you told him he couldn't help you, and that you would help yourself and left, that made your father feel very hurt and useless. He thought that a man who could not help his son was a failure. He cried all night one night. He didn't know how to ever make it up to you. This bothered him for a week until he went over to the church and spoke with Pastor Angelo.

"When he came back, his face was different. He asked me to get his supper and sit and eat with him. Finally, I asked him what had happened, and he said he told the Pastor everything. Then he looked up at me and said all excited, 'I can't give my son everything he wants, but God can!' From that day on, Carlos, your father spent at least thirty minutes a day praying to God for you. He never missed a day."

"When you would call or write and tell me about your hardships in the military or in school or when you looked for the right job, your dad was there. He would ask me how you were, and then he'd go pray. Carlos, He would always pray for you a good wife and for you to have a blessed life. You know, before he died, he started to spend more and more time in prayer. I was telling Pastor Angelo today that I thought he died because he spent so much time talking to God that He took him to heaven to always have him around.

"This was all your father thought he could do for you, and with all your success and all your blessings, all you can do on the day of his burial is still be angry because he couldn't afford to send you to college. His secret desire was that you, too, would learn that no matter how hard a man works, if a man does not have the blessing of God, his labor is in vain!" Having said all this, Lucita quietly left the car and went into her place.

The ride home for Carlos and Evelyn was very quiet. They had nothing to say. All the words of Mama Lucita kept ringing in their head.

When they got home, Carlos walked off to his den and immediately poured himself a drink. He went and sat down, rapt in thought about his father Juan Felipé. He began to reminisce about the events of his life over the past fifteen years. At times, he would break the silence with moans and gestures of realization. Finally, his head lowered with awe and understanding, that divine intervention had to have played a part in his life.

At that moment, Evelyn walked in and said, "Carlos, someday, we will have a child, and we can give that child everything the child could want, but what I want to know is, are we going to give our child what is needed?!"

Carlos understood her point and nodded. As Evelyn left, Carlos turned toward the window and looked toward the sky. He closed his eyes, knelt down on his knees, and began to pray!

Chapter 2

The rainfall that began as a drizzle at the conclusion of Juan Felipé's funeral had now increased to a rainstorm.

Carlos, who began on his knees praying unto God, was now prostate on the floor, slobbering and choked up with tears. He then started confessing and admitting all his faults, he began, "God, I'm the jerk here! Fifteen years didn't have to go by with no relationship with my dad. I wanted to prove to him I could do it all on my own. I realize now I never did. You helped me all along the way. Now, I can never apologize to him!" Carlos continued his breakdown in hard crying and tears.

The rains suddenly became torrential. Lightning flashed, Thunder crashed and then increased as Carlos kept on getting his cry out. As the storm continued, the rolling thunder became louder, as if getting closer. This alarmed Evelyn who began to move quickly through the house to get to Carlos. Her pounding, approaching footsteps made Carlos aware that he was not paying attention to the powerful storm that was just outside, so he began to pick himself up off the floor and collect himself.

"Carlos, this storm is getting loud and heavier!"

As she walked into the den, she noticed Carlos arising from the floor, wiping his face, blowing his nose, and adjusting himself as if nothing happened. Looking at Evelyn, Carlos tried to portray that he was calm and collected. Evelyn looked him over and asked, "Are you all right?"

"Yeah, I was just getting my cry out, finally really thinking about my dad."

"Carlos, I don't think I'll ever forget what your mother said about your dad!"

"I won't either. I realize it was my fault we didn't communicate. I wanted to show him I was better than him, but that was what he wanted. He wanted me to be better than him! Now I realize, I never did do that. In order for me to do that, I now have to start doing like him."

"What do you mean, Carlos? You mean going to church, or doing good things for people like he did?"

"No, Evelyn…if he wanted me to learn anything that he learned in life that was most important, he wanted me to learn to pray to God! Pray for everyone, pray for everything, to allow God to be personally involved in everything in my life. That His Will would be done."

"Okay, Carlos, but where are you going to find the time? You are a busy man with a schedule and responsibilities? You don't' have thirty minutes every day!"

"First, I just want to be faithful in doing. I have you and my mother to pray for, myself and my job as well. I have to talk to Pastor Angelo too. He said he attributed part of his success for the last fifteen years to my father's prayers. I've got to know what that means and experience that kind of success!"

"You better call him now! I'll get you his phone number."

"Thanks. I hope he'll talk to me. I was very rude to him today."

"He wanted to talk to you about your dad and your attitude!"

"Sorry, honey, I did lose my cool back there. Let me call him now." Carlos dialed the number and waited for an answer. "Hello, Pastor Angelo, this is Carlos."

"Hello Carlos, how happy I am you called. It's raining cats and dogs out there. Is everything all right?"

"Yes, Pastor Angelo, I'm sorry about my attitude earlier today, but I do want to sit down and talk with you about my father."

"Well…this is an answer to one of your father's prayers. Carlos, I don't think tonight is a good night for you to be driving around, but tomorrow, you and Evelyn are certainly invited over for dinner with me and my wife. I'll tell her right now. Is six o'clock in the evening good for both of you two?"

"That would be fine. I'll tell Evelyn and we'll be there. See you tomorrow night!" Carlos hung up the phone and turned to Evelyn.

"I look forward to spending time with them, his wife Sister Maria, she is very kind and thoughtful," Evelyn remarked.

Carlos shook his head quickly in agreement, "Yeah, this is company at another level…the family of God level!"

*****

Dinner at the Parsonage

The following evening came quickly. Carlos and Evelyn stayed home due to their company's funeral family benefit and tried to reach Mama Lucita. They found out she had been informed by Pastor Angelo and Sister Maria that they were expected for dinner. Lucita helped Sister Maria prepare the meal, and Evelyn coordinated with them via phone calls to prepare the dessert entrée.

As the hour approached for dinner, Carlos called to announce that they were on their way. Pastor Angelo waited for them in his driveway for their arrival. Pulling up to the parsonage, Pastor Angelo greeted them and welcomed them to his home. Pleasantries were shared, and they were directed to enter into the parsonage. Going inside, Lucita kissed her son and warmly hugged Evelyn, who then led them to the dining room where they all sat and got comfortable.

Pastor Angelo declared, "I hope you all are ready to eat because everything is prepared." Just then, Sister Maria enters the dining area and removes the cake and the tray it was on from the table that Evelyn prepared.

Sister Maria nodded and said, "Thank you," to Evelyn. As she departed back to the kitchen, she began to quietly mutter a prayer in an unknown tongue.[1]

Pastor Angelo, willing to waste no time, said, "Let's eat!"

Sister Maria and Lucita then began bringing in the entrees of food for dinner. There was seasoned chicken breast, mashed potatoes, corn on the cob, buttered broccoli, and fresh baked bread, also included was a large bowl of salad prepared with a colorful array of vegetables, including slices of boiled egg. The smell, as it wafted into everyone's noses, made them enjoy the deep breath it caused.

Pastor Angelo broke the silence by commenting, "When I was growing up, all we cared about was, does it taste good? Today, people worry about calories. Is it keto? How many carbs is this? Is this high glycemic?"

Carlos joined in, "Today, people are more health conscious and *are* concerned about their weight."

"Hogwash!" Pastor Angelo interrupted. "Their problem is, they don't give thanks to God who provided all things!"

Evelyn joined the ladies, bringing forth the food from the kitchen, so as they arrived to complete the table of food, Pastor Angelo motioned for them to remain still and said, "Let's ask the Lord's blessing."

Right then, Carlos and Evelyn noticed how serious everyone was when a word of prayer was uttered. "Let's bow our heads. Father,

---

[1] One of the many manifested gifts of the Holy Spirit, described in 1 Corinthians chapter 12, of the Holy Bible.

we thank you for providing these, thy gifts, for our consumption. We ask you to bless it and nourish our bodies, and use our bodies for your service. In Jesus' name I pray..."

Then all said in unison with the pastor, "Amen!"

Everyone thoroughly enjoyed their meal. During the meal, not much conversation ensued, but a lot of moans and gestures of delight were evident. When they all finished, the ladies cleared the table of all the food and dishes and went to the kitchen to slice the cake Evelyn made for dessert. They took their time because they wanted to give Carlos plenty of time with Pastor Angelo.

Carlos then began opening up to Pastor Angelo. "Pastor, I am now aware that the desire of my father was that, like him, I would learn to pray and allow God total access and involvement in my life. He couldn't give me everything I thought I needed, but God could and did. I realize I'm not just a lucky guy or a skilled businessman or a fortunate husband. All that is the result of a praying father who cared more for me than I ever thought was possible by him and by a merciful God. I thought I was better than him, but now, I just want to be like him."

"This is very enlightening and pleasant to hear, Carlos!" Pastor Angelo responded. "I miss your father, but he had enough foresight to pray and ask of God to send me you. His prayer for you, Carlos, was for you to be a man of God. But every child of God has to start their walk of obedience at the same place."

"And where is that pastor?" Carlos asked.

"At the cross, where our Lord was crucified. You must continually submit your will to His, be obedient to him, listen to Him, cleave to Him, He will never leave you, nor forsake you, Carlos. Then you can know and trust that He will always hear and respond to your prayer. It all begins with your prayer to accept Jesus Christ as your Lord and Savior and to repent of your sins. He will write your name in the Book of Life that you may abide with him forever."

"Pastor, I was praying last night, oh, how I was praying last..." Carlos began to say.

"I'm sure He heard you, Carlos, but the requirement is to first repent of your sins and accept Him as your Lord, Savior, and King!" Pastor Angelo interrupted.

"Then I have to start praying now," Carlos said, and he bowed his head.

Realizing the greatness of the moment, Pastor Angelo extended over the dining table and grabbed Carlos' hands to agree with him as he prayed.

"God, forgive me of all my sins. I never thought of myself as a great sinner, but the sin I have committed was enough for your son Jesus to have to willingly sacrifice himself on a cross to allow me to have access to you, a just and holy God. I accept your Son Jesus as my Lord and Savior. I lost my dad, God, and I thought I was better than him, but now, I find myself wanting to be just like him. When we did talk, he was always teaching me something, but we hadn't talked for fifteen years, and he still wound up teaching me something most important. A man must seek you in prayer and obtain your approval and blessing over everything he does. So, God, I want to know you, the God who blessed my father. Amen."

Pastor Angelo, still stood holding Carlos' hands and saw him beginning to cry. "Very well said Carlos, and God has regarded your confession and also heard your petition. I believe, and your father often prayed, that God has called you for His service."

Pastor Angelo walked around the table to sit next to Carlos and spoke to him. Carlos raised his head and tried to collect himself from being overwhelmed with intense emotion.

Pastor began speaking, "Carlos, you are welcome at our church, and I encourage you to read God's Word daily. Know it! Live it! Be it! I pray, right now, in the name of Jesus, for you to receive the Holy Ghost!"

Carlos humbly bowed his head again.

"Remember also, Carlos, that the saints are not perfect…but are being perfected. It is all our duty to help, encourage, build up, and support one another. It is obvious to me that there is an anointing on your life for service before God. I will personally inform you of opportunity as it's needed."

"Pastor Angelo," Carlos responded, "I really don't know anybody in your church. I'm aware of the challenges for a new leader."

"Carlos, you may not know everyone at my church, but they all know about you," Pastor Angelo interjected. "Your father often spoke to everyone about you. Over the years, he would even brag on you. He was very proud of you! He talked with joy about how God was blessing your life."

"Yeah, Mama was telling me yesterday how Dad stayed behind the scenes, yet he would stay informed about me and go and pray. He made sure God made all the difference," Carlos responded.

Pastor Angelo began emphasizing the following: "You're now beginning to see the impact your father had because he prayed for you, but he impacted many lives. I pray right now that you, too, will experience the joy of fellowship with God Almighty and the undeniable peace of answered prayer because you, too, will stand in the gap and care and pray!"

"That is the success I want to experience!" Carlos acknowledged.

Just then, an outburst of laughter and clapping was coming from the kitchen where the ladies were. Mama Lucita opened the door to announce what happened. As the door was held open, Evelyn and Sister Maria held a prayer circle and were speaking in other tongues in prayer. Mama Lucita excitedly declared, "Evelyn received the Lord Jesus and was baptized in the Holy Spirit!"

Pastor Angelo grabbed Carlos' hand and said, "This is an amazing day! I welcome you and Evelyn today into the kingdom of God!"

There was much discussion afterward of what had transpired that night. Much thanksgiving was continuously being said to God for the evening and its events.

Carlos and Evelyn drove Mama Lucita home that evening, and the conversation was much livelier this time as they rode in the car. Before Mama Lucita exited the car, she said to Carlos, "I hope you now understand that your father really loved you."

"I do, and I really do miss him now, Mama!" Carlos said regretfully.

"Don't worry. You will certainly see him again one day. I'm waiting for that day too!" Mama said, as a matter of fact, before she turned; and she departed inside her home.

The ride home for the two of them forced a grin because they recognized that divine providence had ordained all the sequence of events. As they neared their home and pulled into the garage, Carlos turned to Evelyn and said, "You remember last night that you were asking me if I would give our child what it needs?"

"Yeah, but what makes you bring that up now?" Evelyn asked.

"Well, I think that's what we need right now. But it can only happen if you give me what I want right now," Carlos slyly stated and winked.

Evelyn finally caught the drift.

So Carlos told her, "Wait right there." Carlos rushed out the car and got around to her side and scooped her up like he did on their wedding night, kissing her as he carried her into the house.

Carlos wants to have a family!

Chapter 3

Six months had passed on by, and Carlos and Evelyn were actively participating in church activity, in worship, studying the Word of God, and attending prayer meetings for the church's outreach needs and for the blessing of a revival. Carlos was pouring daily into reading Holy Scripture and kept in touch with Pastor Angelo for wise counsel and fellowship. Evelyn was now twenty-four weeks pregnant, so Carlos prepared breakfast for them both, and they ate. Afterward, as Evelyn prepared to get ready for church that day, Carlos went, as was his new habit, to his den, to pray.

"Heavenly Father, I approach you in the name of Jesus in prayer for the events of this day. I want to thank you again for your care for my mother. She's healthy and well, and she has been surrounded by the care of all the sisters at the church so she never feels alone. Evelyn is now six months pregnant, and it's great to see her happy and still looking radiant. Father, I pray for our child, that as you would bestow blessings and favor, you would also instill an understanding heart to obey you in every decision they make. Watch over every employee in my company, allowing them safe travel to work and home, and help them to do their jobs with confidence and care for every detail. And, Father, we have been praying for revival, revival in our church, revival in our city, revival in our state, revival in our nation. Let your church, Lord, experience revival throughout the world, in all its churches, in all their meetings wherever they gather, that all may know you are a God that can make dead things live again. I wrote that in a song I was penning to use to worship you with privately in my prayers, Father! Lastly, I wanted to ask again for your anointing to fall afresh upon Pastor Angelo as he ministers the Word of God today. May lives be revived, the backslider restored to obey you again, them who are lost—to be redeemed today, and any feeling ill, that they may approach you with faith to believe, pray, and be healed. Thank you, Father. I ask all these things in Jesus's name, amen."

Carlos arose from his knees and made his way through his home to check on Evelyn, seeing her, he stared and said, "I still have the hots for my wife!"

"Stop it!" Evelyn tried to explain. "I have to buy more maternity dresses, and this is already fitting tight and uncomfortable."

"But it looks good on you, Ev. It looks good on you!" Carlos kept staring at her as she walked by him to get her shoes. Just then, the phone rang; Carlos went to answer, still staring at Evelyn. The phone kept ringing, so Carlos reluctantly answered it for interrupting his moment.

"Hello? Oh, Pastor Angelo, what can I do for you? Ev and I are getting ready to leave now to church."

Pastor Angelo explained his call. "Glad I caught you before you left, Carlos. I didn't want you to be surprised by anything this morning."

Evelyn turned to look at Carlos and saw his face change, so she thought something was wrong; she approached and stood next to Carlos. Carlos' stare changed to a look of expecting the worst and asked, "Is anything wrong, Pastor?"

"No, Carlos," Pastor responded immediately to ease Carlos' concern. "Brother and Sister Thomas went on vacation and won't be in attendance today. What I need is for you to oversee the youth and children's Sunday school classes. Don't worry about youth and children's church today. We will have them all assemble with the adults today for church."

"What lesson will I use for instruction today or what have they been studying lately that I can continue in during the time?" Carlos asked, all puzzled.

"That won't be necessary, Carlos, you basically are going to be a glorified babysitter till the morning worship service begins with the adults. You can sing songs or have a testimony time and share a word of prayer with them. You want to keep them occupied till it's time to start the adult service together with them. Can you handle this? If not, I can always ask—" Pastor Angelo rolled on.

"I can do it!" Carlos assured Pastor Angelo as he interrupted him.

"Great, then I'll see you at church!" Pastor said as he hung up.

Evelyn kept staring at Carlos now to have an explanation for the phone call. Carlos slowly turned away to hang up the phone with a look of bewilderment on his face and he said, "Pastor wants me to oversee the youth and children's Sunday school classes today because the Thomases are away on vacation."

"Ohhh, I thought something bad had happened. Carlos, not to worry, I'm sure the lesson for today's class won't be difficult to conduct and instruct," Evelyn said, trying to encourage Carlos.

"No, Ev, that's not it at all. There's no lesson to teach. I'm basically being a babysitter for the class time until we all assemble together for worship this morning," Carlos said, bearing a worried expression. "I think their time spent at church is as important as any adults attending."

"They are, Carlos, and I will 'babysit' with you. We can interact with them together," Evelyn said to alleviate the weight of worry Carlos appeared to be bearing alone.

"Thanks, that helps a lot. But first, let's have a moment of prayer specifically for this!" Carlos insisted.

Evelyn stepped to stand face-to-face with Carlos and reached to grab his extended arms to pray. Carlos began by telling Evelyn, "Agree with me as we pray." She nodded agreeably and closed her eyes as Carlos started, "Father, Ev and I come to you in Jesus' name, praying in behalf of our youth and young children that she and I will be overseeing this morning. God, I know that each of these young people have cares and concerns just like us adults, and I'm praying now for them to have a very real and personal experience with You today. Make them know they are useful, and if they are willing, great things *can* be accomplished through their efforts. Manifest your power and greatness before them today..." As Carlos continued praying, suddenly, the Holy Spirit was stirred up within Evelyn, and she began to loudly pray with Carlos in an unknown tongue.[2] Carlos continued with his petition. "Let every young person experience your personal presence in their lives today, and may it have an effect for lifelong good. To your honor and praise and glory in Jesus' name I pray..."

Just then, Evelyn stopped praying in an unknown tongue and calmly asked the Spirit of God to interpret her utterance.[3] She then clearly stated, "I have heard your prayer and will manifest my power today in their presence by my Spirit!"

---

[2] One of many manifested gifts of the Holy Spirit listed in 1 Corinthians 12.

[3] Another manifested gift of the Holy Spirit assigned to some believers listed in 1 Corinthians 12.

Carlos stared at Evelyn with joy at the interpretation of her prayer, and the word of knowledge[4] that was also given so he enthusiastically concluded praying with an extended, "Aaaamen!"

Knowing Carlos was encouraged, Evelyn went to her closet to find the pair of shoes she would wear. "Carlos, don't expect me to be wearing high heels anymore. Low heels or flats from now on. I want to be comfortable."

Carlos returned to his attracted stare, saying, "You look good in anything you wear! Let me tie my tie, and we can go to churrrch!"

Arriving at the church, Carlos now understood Evelyn's shoes were uncomfortable on her feet, so he had her sit till he came around and opened the door for her and took her hand and escorted her inside. They went downstairs, for the classrooms were down there, and began grabbing chairs and set them up in the central hall there by the baptistery for when the youth members arrive.

"Ev, you don't have to help with the chairs." Carlos was trying to be considerate to his pregnant wife.

"I'm here to help you, Carlos," she said, appreciating his noble gesture. "What would you like me to do then?"

"Well, we are going to be doing some singing, so you can play the piano, but right now, you can greet them as they come in, and I'll set up the chairs," Carlos said as he tries to organize the seating arrangement and finish grabbing all the chairs. Carlos moved as quickly as he could, and when he finished the arrangement, he went and stood with Evelyn to greet each one as they arrived and came downstairs. Carlos began telling them all as they arrived to take a seat in the open hall there by the baptistery. He explained that Bro. and Sis. Thomas went on vacation, and that they were all going to take time to share testimonies and later sing some songs. He also told them that they would participate in worship with the adults later in the morning.

---

[4] Another distinct gift of the Holy Spirit also listed in 1 Corinthians 12 by Apostle Paul.

When he finished explaining and returned to Evelyn's side by the doorway, just then, Sister Edna Boyce came in with her son Eddy-Boy (called such because he was Edward Boyce Jr). He was visibly upset and told his mother that he didn't want to be there at church.

Carlos and Evelyn couldn't help but eavesdrop their conversation. Evelyn then went to gather with the others seated and took her place by the piano.

"Don't worry, Mom, I'll find a way to make money and take care of you," Eddy-Boy spurted in bitter anger.

"Oh, Eddy-Boy, we will be all right. Now go downstairs and attend your class, but we are staying here at church this morning!" Sister Edna tried consoling her son. He reluctantly went down the stairs where Carlos waited for him.

Carlos tried to ease the mood with a hip, nice-to-see-you welcome, "What's up, Eddy-Boy?!"

"Ain't nothing up right now. In fact, ain't nothing good either," Eddy-Boy responded as he saw everyone sitting in arranged seats by the baptistery. Eddy-Boy tried to walk right by Carlos, but Carlos stepped in his way.

"You want to tell me, man-to-man, what's going on that has you on ten!" Carlos used the right words to get Eddy-Boy to talk about it, for he was young, wanting to be a man, so he opened up to Carlos.

"It's my dad! He's moved out and not going to help my mom anymore. He wants a divorce and told her he'll pay support when ordered by the court." Eddy-Boy laid it out for Carlos and finished by saying, "I'll be better than him, I'll make money and take care of my mom!"

Carlos knew how those shoes fit. It struck a chord in him, so he compassionately responded, "I was just like you. I didn't talk to my dad for fifteen years, then he died. It wasn't till after we buried him that my mother told me that even though I wouldn't talk to him, he always wanted to know what was going on in my life, then he'd go pray. I wanted to be better than him too! Thought I was better than him. I had a better job, made more money, beautiful wife. But what I didn't know then was he wanted me to be better than him. He asked God every day for that. What I want to ask of you is to trust God.

Let's try Him at His Word. He says ask, seek, and knock.[5] I want you to pray with me to ask God to restore your family back together, that you will seek to know him intimately, in a personal way, in all of your life, and lastly, that you're knocking on His door, for God to open the opportunity for this to happen."

Eddy-Boy looked at Carlos and smiled, realizing the test was on God to prove His Word is true. Eddy-Boy then says, "Okay, let's ask."

Carlos wrapped his arm around Eddy-Boy's shoulder and led in prayer. When they finished, they went and joined everyone else, and Carlos began to lead the morning's event with an upbeat tone so everybody felt comfortable with each other.

"Good morning, everyone. You all may know me. I'm Carlos, or know of me, but I have yet to meet and know all of you. At the piano is my pretty and pregnant wife Evelyn. So now, we are going to start going around the room, giving everyone the opportunity to introduce themselves and share a testimony of something good God has done in your life. We'll start right here with you, Donna."

Donna wasn't surprised by being picked first. "Hi, I'm Donna. You all know me, and yes, I do have a testimony to share. God has been helping me to excel in all my classes, and I am again on the honor Roll with straight A grades and perfect attendance."

"Thank you, Donna, *that* is what every student wants and where everyone wants to be, at the top of their class." Carlos looked around at the young men and continued. "Let's have a young man next, you sir. Tell us your name and share a testimony, if you have one that brags on Jesus."

"My name is Timothy, and my testimony is, my dad taught me how to string a line on my pole, attach my hook and bait, cast my line and wait patiently for the fish to bite, and reel them in. Dad told me now that I know how to fish, I can eat forever. Thank you, Jesus!"

Everyone couldn't help but loudly chuckle after hearing Timothy's testimony.

Carlos added, "Very good, Timothy, and perhaps now your new testimony will be that you've become a great fisher of men for God."

---

[5] Matthew 7:7, direct words from the Lord Jesus Christ.

Carlos looked at the clock on the wall and wanted to move to the next thing he was asked to do by Pastor Angelo, so he asked, "Is there anybody else that would love to share a testimony and introduce themselves?"

Unexpectedly, Eddy-Boy stood from his chair and said, "I do, my name is Edward Boyce Jr., you can call me Eddy-Boy. I really feel like I can't trust nobody, but today, I decided to trust God. I'm keeping my word, so I expect Him to keep His."

"That's great, Eddy-Boy, just remember, when an opportunity to do good comes, don't wait for an invitation. Step up and do the good thing! You know what I mean?" Carlos asked.

Eddy-Boy nodded his head and sat back down.

Carlos changed the subject and said, "I want us now to learn this song that I've written to sing in my private worship. I'm sharing it with you because you might find it useful to sing when you pray or walk along your way. But first we have to separate into groups like a choir. You know, bass, tenor, soprano, and alto. We'll start by having each of you sing a single word, *praise*. Then we'll know where you need to be."

Carlos had them line up before the piano Evelyn was at, and she would cue them to sing and adjust an octave to test for their range. Carlos put them in their proper groups, and it appeared they were all evenly numbered. Last in line was Eddy-Boy, and he appeared to have a matured voice and sound.

Evelyn looked at Carlos and said, "Baritone."

"Wow!" Carlos said. "You stand up front, to the side of the tenors."

Evelyn agreed and shook her head so. "Okay, I have four verses to this song that I will sing. We will now rehearse the chorus and get you familiar with it."

Evelyn went through each group, helping them to maintain their tone and pitch, and they wonderfully blended well when they sang in unison. So Carlos was ready to lead them through the song. As they began, Pastor Angelo came walking through and stopped to listen for a moment. Carlos began his introduction, and when the chorus line approached and the young men sang, Pastor Angelo was pleasantly shocked, but when the young women began to release their peals, Pastor Angelo had to interrupt.

"Excuse me, Carlos, what song is that you all are singing?" the pastor enquired.

"This is a song I wrote that I sing in my private devotional prayer and worship. I shared with them to have something creative to do while we wait together till morning service," Carlos noted.

Pastor Angelo thought for a moment then stated, "This is truly divine, and you must share this song in morning worship later. Can you all do this?" Everybody nodded and agreed, happy they were able to contribute that morning. "Carlos, I'll leave you to continue rehearsing."

"All right, I believe we'll be ready. It's a simple chorus, giving God the highest praise!" Carlos was thankful he was able to participate with the youth. As the pastor departed, Carlos continued his rehearsal till he felt they were ready and then had everyone huddle around him, and he pointed out his hand signals to conduct them all understandably. Then he led them in a prayer, thanking each of them.

As everyone began to put all the chairs back in their classrooms, Carlos grabbed Eddy-Boy and told him, "There's one part of the chorus I didn't share with everyone except you. Here it is. It's sang seven times in the same timeframe as the original praise in the chorus. It's my original conclusion to this song. I want you to sing it when you feel it's time to kick up the worship to God to the ultimate level. You got it?"

"Yeah, I'll try my best," Eddy-Boy said, trying to be confident.

*****

The service started as normal. Announcements were made, and the offering was taken, then Pastor Angelo approached the pulpit and informed the congregation, "This morning's service has been altered for a variety of reasons, some of which many of you all are aware of, and the rest of you are not. I want to be obedient to the Spirit of God this morning and introduce a change for this morning's service.

We'll begin with a song of praise and worship, led and performed by Carlos and his wife Evelyn and the members of our youth and children's ministries. Would you all approach the platform and present your offering?"

As Evelyn helped conduct the singers to their arranged positions, Carlos grabbed the microphone and began to explain, "This song that I shared today with our youth, I wrote for private worship in my devotional time. I wanted to give the Lord my highest praise, for He is worthy. Worship with us as we sing." Carlos begins singing, "Praise…"[6]

---

[6] Carlos began singing the author's song, "Praise! To His Eternal Holiness!" Content included at back of book.

As the young people all began to join in singing and the congregation was being moved by the Spirit of the Lord, Eddy-Boy's father walked into the service looking for Edna and sat right next to her, giving the pretense that he was staying for the worship service. They begin having a discussion in the pew. Edna turned and questioned him, asking, "What are you doing here?"

Edward[7] saw that he had to come clean, so he tried to lower his voice and confessed, "I want to come back home. I was in an affair that failed." Edward motioned his hands down, trying to get Edna not to create a scene.

Edna, being filled with embarrassment and anger, shook her head resolutely to reinforce her response and said, "No!" and turned her face away from him.

Edward lost face, but he tried to collect himself so as not to make a scene. He rose to leave the sanctuary, which Eddy-Boy witnessed and it tore him at his heart. Eddy-Boy lifted his gaze toward heaven and told God in his heart that he's still knocking for opportunity to have his family restored as he signified this by raising his hand and knocking. Eddy-Boy stepped forward with uplifted arms and began to belt out the final chorus. Evelyn and Carlos were taken by surprise but kept the chorus moving by directing the singers to follow through with the remainder of the chorus line.

Edward Boyce, just before exiting the sanctuary, recognizes that it's his son singing at the top of his lungs, and it moved his heart. He turned and looked directly at Eddy-Boy singing, and he decided to make his way to the altar to pray. Pastor Angelo saw this and met him there for prayer. Edward approached and opened up, confessing his faults to the pastor before the Lord and the church, then bowed down and wept. Pastor stood behind Edward and laid his hands on his shoulders and prays for him. Edna, having witnessed all this, rose from her pew and came forth to the altar in tears and declared out loud that she forgave him. Edward lifted his head and looked on Edna as she arrived. She saw his eyes full of tears, and they hugged

---

[7] Edward Boyce Sr. was an attendee of this church till his secret affair began.

each other. Eddy-Boy rejoiced on the platform by looking toward heaven and jumping for joy.

With great joy evident throughout the church, Pastor Angelo asked Carlos to sing the song one more time. Before Carlos led the choir back into song, he paced back and forth before the platform, saying out loud, "Out of the mouth of babes you have ordained strength!"[8] Carlos then began signaling to Evelyn and the Choir to resume the song from the start. Among all the pews, everyone sang and danced and swayed with arms waved unto the Lord in worship. It was an unforgettable moment for them all. The presence of God was experienced by all!

When the song finally concluded and the congregation took their seats, Pastor Angelo returned to the pulpit. "I have a few more things to say today. It feels genuinely satisfying to obey the leading of the Holy Spirit!" The parishioners agreed and affirmed his statement with a hearty "Amen."

As the choir dispersed into their seats, Eddy-Boy went and hugged his dad and sat very close to him in the pew with great joy.

Pastor Angelo continued, "Well, it seems I should start with a big one we have today, the restoration of a man to his family. We are beginning to see the revival you all pray for. Where fathers are restored to their sons and sons to their fathers."

The church rejoices. Carlos looked right at Eddy-Boy and told him, "You didn't hesitate to do that good thing!"

Eddy-Boy shook his head in agreement and hugged his dad.

Pastor caught up with Carlos as he was leaving Sunday's service and seating Evelyn in her seat in the car. He asked Carlos for a minute to talk. They both stopped and stood in front of his car.

"Carlos, I am sincerely impressed by the anointing of God on your life. You are allowing God to be God over every *detail of* your life! Your father prayed for such a thing. I'm thankful to witness it!" Pastor Angelo shared all excitedly.

"Pastor, I realize the abundance of blessings in my life are the result of a loving father who faithfully prayed for his son that God

---

[8] Psalm 8:2.

would provide, and He did. But I learned that in praying like my father did, although many blessings are nice to have, the thing that excites me the most every day, is the privilege that I have to go and commune with God and have a personal audience in worship to our Creator," Carlos said with conviction.

"You definitely are a man after God's own heart, Carlos," Pastor affirmed.

"The Lord is my Shepherd… He leads me… I will follow Him," Carlos responded and went to get into his car and then drive away.

Pastor Angelo kept watching Carlos and Evelyn as they departed in their car and moved farther away. He then turned his gaze toward heaven and began speaking to God, "I know you have anointed Carlos for a great work for you. It is amazing to see Your Holy Spirit operating in his life. I thank You for answering the prayer of his father. Juan Felipé trusted You to help his son. Now You will use him to help many. Thank You! It's exciting to see the work of God in one's life. Carlos, God be with you and Evelyn." Pastor kept watching them as they continued to drive away.

Chapter 4

About this same time, fifteen years earlier, Juan Felipé got up and was purposed to make his way downtown to a Christian bookstore. Upon arriving there, he began to browse a little while till he found a staff person who finally became available and let her know he was needing some assistance. She happily greeted Juan Felipé and enquired as to what exactly it was he was looking for.

"Welcome to our store. My name is Deborah and you can call me Debbie. What can I help you with today? I pray we have exactly what you need from the Lord to help you in your daily walk with Him."

"This is not for me, but it would be a gift for my son who already left and joined the military. He's a Marine," Juan Felipé said, realizing he was now speaking with a tone of pride.

"Well, this is fantastic!" Debbie said. "What do you want to get him, some music to listen to, or how about a good book to read? I have some neat fictional storybooks that I'm sure he would enjoy reading in his free time—"

"No!" Juan Felipé said, cutting her off from completing her list of choices. "I want to buy him a Bible, a good one, one that will help him understand it well."

"I see now. What it is you are wanting is a study Bible. You are blessed because we have a variety of them to choose from. Come over here to see their displays. We have them in paperback, hardcover, like in school, and then we also have them leather-bound, like a minister would want, to share the Word of God with. Which one would you like to get him?" Debbie excitedly said, knowing she had his interest piqued by the many on display to look at.

Juan Felipé' didn't even look toward the selection of paperback nor hardcover copies of scripture that were displayed but rather stepped up to the area where the leather-bound copies were displayed and asked Debbie, "What is the best one that you have?"

"Really, sir, that is a matter of opinion." Debbie tried to calmly further explain to Juan Felipé. "Professors in all Bible colleges have a different opinion, and all recommend different ones that better relate to their course of study by their content of commentary or concordance and maps. They also look at…"

As she continued explaining, Juan Felipé started walking before the many that were displayed and simply was looking at their size and noticed the content detailed on the spine as Debbie was continuing her discussion on them. Juan Felipé's eye then just took notice of one that stood out to him because of its particular size. It wasn't small, but it wasn't large like some that were on display. He was thinking Carlos needed something that had study content, for Juan Felipé wanted Carlos to know the Word of God but not bulky so he could carry it with him wherever he went. Debbie was still explaining to Juan Felipé as he walked further on and stopped, then pointed and said, "That one. That's the one!"

That's the one!

"Oh, wow!" Debbie said, amazed at his choice. "You selected a classic study Bible. That is a Thompson, Chain-Reference Study Bible! We also have currently an additional promotion for Bibles purchased at this time. We will engrave the name of your son on its cover so no one can ever be confused as to who is the owner of it. Just give me his name, and we will engrave it in gold lettering on the cover. I'll even wrap it for you so it will be ready for shipping. So just give me his name…"

Juan Felipé was suddenly hit with the awareness of how beautiful and powerful this gift was for his son, so with his eyes beginning to water, he proudly walked over to her at her counter and said to Debbie, "Carlos DeLeon, C-A-R-L-O-S D-E-L-E-O-N! Please, have it all in capitals."

*****

Juan Felipé arrived home, and Lucita had lunch ready and was waiting for him to arrive. He sat down to eat and placed a wrapped package on the table next to his plate. When Lucita came with the lunch she prepared and began to serve Juan Felipé, she noticed the package and thought initially that it was a gift for her. So after she sat down and Juan Felipé asked the Lord for his blessing on the meal and thanked Him for it, Lucita smiled and asked, "What did you get for me? And why?"

Juan Felipé suddenly looked upon Lucita sadly and said, "It's not for you." As he saw her face change he informed her, "It's not for me either." He then felt compelled to explain, "I'm sorry, Mama, and I didn't let you know where I went and what I was going to do. I went today to buy Carlos a Bible. It's a Study Bible. I want him to know the Word of God. There were even bigger ones I could have chosen, but I wanted to get him one that he could take and carry with him everywhere. The next time you speak to him, I want you to make him promise that he will always carry this with him and read it too! I want you to send this to him after lunch."

Lucita was all excited about it all and shook her head gladly and said, "I will!"

"I even was able to have his name engraved on it in gold-lettering," Juan Felipé said proudly. "Just don't tell Carlos that I bought it for him. Tell him you did."

The two of them then went and continued their meal knowing they had provided something for Carlos that he could have and treasure for life. Now when they finished their meal, and Lucita began taking their plates off the table, the phone began ringing. Lucita calmly told Juan Felipé, "I'll get it." knowing he was all full from his meal. When she answered the phone, Juan Felipé, who was still at the table, could hear a lot of background noise on the phone. Lucita began asking, "What is this noise? Who is this calling?"

Just then, Carlos began speaking loudly to overcome the background noise, "Hey, Mama, it's me, Carlos. We just got orders. We're being deployed!"

Lucita responded with surprise, "Deployed?"

"Yeah, Mama, we got a lot of activity over here. We're getting ready to move out. We're going to the Middle East!" Carlos was trying to speak clearly.

"Mi precioso hijo!"[9] Lucita started to worry. "Let me call your father and tell him."

"No, Mama," Carlos came right back, responding, "I don't want to talk to him. I'll be all right. Listen, Mama, I'm trained for this!"

Lucita didn't want to forget about Carlos' gift so she said to him, "Mijo,[10] I want you to promise me something."

"Anything, Mama, I'm 'gonna' come back home!" Carlos tried to assure his mother.

"I'm sending you a Bible, I want you to take it with you everywhere you go and read it too! Now promise me!" Lucita demanded.

Carlos was surprised and pleased, saying, "Yeah, Mama, I sure could use one. I'll take good care of it! I 'gotta' go. I will call you once I get settled over there. Goodbye, Mama." Carlos hung up, leaving Lucita in silence.

---

[9] A Spanish phrase that means "My precious son!"
[10] A Spanish term of endearment that means "darling."

Lucita turned around and looked back at Juan Felipé and told him, "Carlos is being deployed to the Middle East. There's a war over there. I told him I'm sending him a Bible. He promised he would keep it with him."

"Go ahead and send it to him. I'm going to go pray," Juan Felipé said while staring at Lucita's worried look, so he continued by saying, "Lucita, you will see him again."

Lucita was encouraged and relieved by his confidence, so she shook her head in agreement, grabbed Carlos' package and departed to ship it. Juan Felipé watched her until she left and went to his bedroom, fell to his knees, and began to pray. "Heavenly Father, I come to you in Jesus' name, your holy son, in behalf of my son Carlos, who has just been deployed to the Middle East. I'm asking for your protection and care for him, and that his mother would see him again, healthy and unharmed. I know and believe that nothing is impossible with you. It's because of this that I have given you my heart and trust you with my life. My son won't speak to me, and it deeply hurts me, but today, Father, I went and bought a study Bible for Carlos. It's an investment of faith. I'm asking you to provide generously and care for all his needs and let all his experiences in life train him and prepare him to be useful to you, to help and bless others. In the Bible, there are stories of parents who offered their children to idols, I'm offering my son to you, my Creator, asking you to create him to be a man after your own heart, and I'm asking *You* to make him a man of God! Let his life be framed with discipline and spiritual gifts, but most importantly, I ask you to give Carlos leadership ability, so his life and actions will lead others to you. Amen."

*****

Carlos had gotten home from work, and Evelyn had a quick and small dinner prepared for them because it was Wednesday; they had to be ready to attend midweek service later that evening. When Carlos arrived, Evelyn was looking forward to hear the new creative affections Carlos would express to her, and he did. He was so attracted to Evelyn and in love with his wife that he was always looking for a new way to express it. As the meal was finished, Carlos continued his playful banter with Evelyn and put a smile on her face as she took the dishes to the kitchen. Carlos was enjoying his view of Evelyn as she departed, when suddenly, he was spellbound in thought for a moment before going to go into his den and pray before heading to midweek service for prayer meeting this evening. His mind kept thinking about the words of Pastor Angelo in that he commented on revival, beginning with the return of Edward Boyce back to his wife and son. Praying for revival was something that was a continuous prayer request and petition at every prayer meeting.

Carlos reached and grabbed his Bible, a Thompson Chain-Reference Bible, which he now treasured because he learned his father bought it, but his mother sent it to him when he went on his first deployment in the military. This Bible traveled with him in all his travels. He kept it with him as a promise to his mother, but now, it is his resource for life. Carlos opened it up and began flipping through to the back of his Thompson Bible to the section marked "Condensed Cyclopedia of Topics and Texts." He began flipping a few pages into it, and his eye immediately caught the topic "Awakenings and Religious Reforms." Looking into it, it began with "(A) Awakenings, Religious." His eye kept scrolling down the content of (A) till he came to the next subtopic: (B) Revivals. He started to go to read the selected passage of Isaiah chapter 35 but then looked at the general referenced verses under point (1), but when he came to the heading of point (2) "Sought," Carlos got encouraged for his discovery and said, "Yes, this is where we are at Lord!" He began reading the listed verses out loud:

> Restore unto me the joy of thy salvation; and uphold me with thy free Spirit. Then will I teach transgressors thy ways; and sinners will be converted unto thee. (Psalms 51:12–13)

> Turn us again, O God of hosts, and cause thy face to shine; and we shall be saved. (Psalms 80:7)

> Wilt thou not revive us again: that thy people may rejoice in thee? (Psalms 85:6)

> Until the Spirit be poured upon us from on high, and the wilderness be a fruitful field, and the fruitful field be counted for a forest. (Isaiah 32:15)

> O Lord, I have heard thy speech, and was
> afraid; O Lord, revive thy work in the midst of
> the years, in wrath remember mercy. (Habakkuk
> 3:2)

Carlos slowly closed his Bible and set it down, realizing that the revival they had been praying for in their meetings was vividly described in Scripture by the psalmist and prophets in those verses as a state where the believer had lost their joy and vitality of spiritual indwelling, had sinned and not held God in the highest regard in all their life because of being distracted. Where the Body was not to be dry and empty, but active and fluidly meeting needs and displaying not only the gifts of the Spirit, but all of its fruits too! It's about living up to the capability given by the Lord of the church.

Carlos began to tearfully and fearfully fall to his knees and pray, "Father, I come before you in Jesus' name with the need to repent. I gather with others every week to pray with one another and for one another, which is good in itself, but then we gather, every week, and conclude our meeting together praying for revival. Father, *we* need to be revived. I know God that you would never deny anyone the blessing of your Spirit, giving us the ability to live life more abundantly, but our hearts have hindered you. We care for too many 'things' in this life, which chokes out our ability to have a genuine godly influence upon others. I know, Father, that many may look upon me because I have a new this, the prettiest wife, or the best that, and I'm thankful that you have provided all these for me to enjoy. But what I want everyone to know is that you are more important to me than any of it! If you want me to get rid of anything, I will. I dedicate all that I have, and my job too, to You and I pray I can use it all for your purposes. So, Father, *I want revival* and let it start in *me*. I am rededicating my life to you. I'm asking you to open my eyes and ears to make me sensitive to the lead of the Holy Spirit. Make me able to consider everything before me with the mind of my anointed Lord, according to your Holy Word. Help me to consider also how *You* look for faith in men and women to believe. I want to be like your holy Son Jesus, going forth obediently, pleasing you in all things. I want to be an obedient son to You Father, maturing into a man of God! For Your honor and glory. Amen."

Carlos fell forward again, this time on his face, prostrate on the floor and banging his fist on the floor with conviction, saying, "Great God, you are what matters…it's all about Your praise! It's all about Your honor! It's all about Your glory! Father, use me to declare this and minister Your grace to everyone who would believe and lead them to trust in You."

Evelyn was ready to go to midweek service and went to Carlos' den to let him know she was ready to go. When she entered and saw Carlos on the floor, she ran to him thinking he was hurt. "Carlos, what happened? Are you okay?" Evelyn began to try to help Carlos up, but he only arose to sit up and turn to face Evelyn. Evelyn grabbed some tissues and began to wipe Carlos' face and hand him some so he could blow his nose and finish cleaning himself up. When he did, with Evelyn watching him, Evelyn asked him again, "Carlos, what happened? We just had an enjoyable moment together at dinner. I know you came here to pray, but I have never seen you like this!" Evelyn curiously asked again.

I surrendered.

"I surrendered," Carlos answered. He then began to fully arise and stand up before Evelyn. He then continued to explain what is happening. He clutched each of her hands and looked into her eyes and spoke, "I came here to pray about revival, like we always do every Wednesday night at midweek service. The Lord led me to read some scriptures listed under that topic, 'Revival,' in the back of my Bible. After reading them, I realized we are not prepared for 'Revival.' In fact, we hinder God because we have become content with the title 'Christian' and lukewarm in our effort to be obedient. Very few are willing to pay the price of tarrying in the presence of God in prayer as an intercessor and worshipping Him with all of their life. Ev, I'm thankful for all that we have, my job too! My Father prayed faithfully for all our blessings, and God generously bestowed all of it upon us. They are enjoyed and appreciated, but our comfort is not as important as the will of God. God wants us restored to Him, living abundantly in obedience! Whenever God wanted to do something great among the people, He always started with a man. Tonight I asked God to be that Man."

Evelyn stood beholding the sincerity of Carlos and expressed back, "I fully support you, Carlos. I'm your wife and soon to be mother of our child. But what am I supposed to do?"

"We will dedicate our child to the Lord and trust Him to help us care for our child. In like manner, we will dedicate ourselves to the Lord and trust Him, we will follow Him, *believing* He will guide us *every step* of the way," Carlos emphasized.

"Then there's something I must do first," Evelyn said, closing her eyes while she gripped Carlos' hands firmer, for him to agree with her in prayer. Carlos held her hands firmly, waiting to know what she had to pray about. "Father, I surrender to you too!"

Carlos was very happy now because he realized he was not alone now. The two of them were now one, in body, in spirit, and in life purpose. Carlos went and grabbed his Bible then took hold of Evelyn's hand again and said, "Let's go to church. We are now ready to go!"

Chapter 5

Discussing the times on the way to church.

Carlos went and had Evelyn seated and got around to his side of the car and sat down. After Carlos started his car with the push of a button and raised his garage door, he paused for a moment; still holding the gear shift, Carlos stayed thinking before proceeding to engage, then let the shifter go. Evelyn noticed and turned and looked at Carlos, wondering what he was waiting for. When Carlos then noticed Evelyn's stare, he began to tell her, "We have been praying and praying for revival every week, but what we haven't done is prepare for the move of God in people's lives! I believe

God is making you and me aware of the need for what he is doing. We are going to have to take a lead in this to help Pastor Angelo and the entire church prepare for growth."

"What exactly should we be preparing for?" Evelyn curiously asked.

"As I recall," Carlos responded, "God already gave us the blueprint. It's in the Book of Acts! There's no telling how great the move of God will be. It may start small in appearance, but it's always huge. Remember?"

"Yeah!" Evelyn shook her head in agreement. "God was adding them into the assembly of believers by the thousands. They had to start meeting in homes."

Carlos began to engage the car in gear and move forward down his driveway. "You're seeing it!" Carlos went on describing. "Everyone began sharing all their possessions, keeping what they had available because they cared about helping each other's needs, knowing the Word of God, and corporate fellowship with each other and with the Holy Spirit. The apostles recognized they couldn't do all things to meet everyone's needs, so once they saw their role, to lead in prayer and the ministry of the Word, they then went and looked for Spirit-filled believing leaders to oversee and administer the commonly shared resources. This was the start, but the church continued to grow! I'm expecting us to grow!" Carlos rolled to the end of his driveway and waited before entering the street to listen to Evelyn, making sure his garage was closed.

"Okay, Carlos, who will oversee these appointments? I don't want to get into arguments with anyone about who is selected to be in charge," Evelyn worriedly said.

"Back to the blueprint, Ev, the apostles had the believers select the most notable of themselves to oversee the needed tasks. This was the start of deacons in the church. As a result, a large number of priests and ministers were moved to greater obedience in the faith. When God moves, it is His will that all, great and small, rich and poor, minister and layman are affected to obedience. Otherwise, the alternative is never desirable." Carlos set his turn signal, looked to make sure the road was clear to proceed, and drove on.

"When you speak of alternative, you're talking about judgment from God, aren't you?" Evelyn surmised.

"Yes, Evelyn," Carlos sadly responded then continued, "It's apparent that we are at the end of His dispensation of Grace toward men. God will bring judgment, and it starts in the house of God. Now I believe God is preparing to pour forth His latter rains of blessing to gather as many will answer His call. Our times are just as predicted in the Scriptures, as told by the apostle Paul to Timothy. He said the Holy Spirit specifically described our times, listen, He said, some would depart from the faith, listening to deceptive spirits and following the teachings of wicked devils, they will tell their lies hypocritically with no regard for them being all wrong. Oh, it gets crazier, Ev, then these backsliders will demand of people to not get married. I'm sure you already saw other people rebuking everyone else just for eating meat, saying it's wrong and harmful, but God says it's okay. All our meals are made acceptable by the Word of God and prayer."

"Uh-huh!" Evelyn agreed. "You know, Carlos, I was just reading the letters to Timothy today. The apostle Paul went into more detail in his second letter!"

"He sure did in chapter 3." Carlos was thankful Evelyn was immediately familiar about what he was speaking about, so he continued, "The apostle Paul quoted the Holy Spirit saying the days would be 'perilous.' We don't even use that word much anymore, but he was saying that these times are going to be full of danger or risk. This lets us know that every devil won't waste a moment trying to make every person a victim of their thievery, murder, or destructive acts. I'm thankful for the protective care of the Lord Jesus, our Great Shepherd, over His flock!"

"Carlos, I'm thankful for the care of the Lord over me, and I know He has protected you. For you to even be home today after being in a war is evidence of His decisive care over you!" Evelyn acknowledged.

"Thank you, there were situations that I know were acts of God, but let's look at what we are going to have to face and minister to people who have been either involved or a victim of..." Carlos continued, "*Extreme selfishness,* people that care nothing for their neighbor. *Greedy people* that want nothing but money or whatever they think is of value to gratify their vices. They will be *boastful, conceited,* and *insulting. Disobedient* to their parents, *unthankful and unholy,* having no religious care. They will be *cruel, slandering,* and *violent,* even hating those that do good. Loving pleasure rather than loving God. They will try and act like they could be godly, but their witness and testimony will not be believable. You can't even be around these people. They will learn many things but never able to acknowledge the truth that they need the salvation and cleansing that only comes from acceptance and submission to the Lord Jesus Christ!"

"Wow, Carlos, you studied that passage well!" Evelyn was surprised at his grasp and recall.

"Every one of these Scriptures is 'God-breathed,'" Carlos said, holding up his Bible, that his dad, Juan Felipé, had provided for him. "This is sooo beneficial and useful to me. It has been teaching me, reproving me, correcting me, and instructing me on what God said is right, maturing me and making me capable to do every task He assigned for me to do." Carlos began pulling into the church parking lot and parked his vehicle. Before getting out, he told Evelyn, "Once I get you seated for tonight, I need to go and speak to Pastor Angelo and share with him about our renewed commitment and what the Lord is leading us to do." Carlos then went and opened her door and escorted her inside to the sanctuary.

Entering into the sanctuary, they were immediately surprised to see the entire Boyce family sitting and waiting as well. All were sharing hellos as Carlos and Evelyn approached and the ladies shared hugs and the men warm handshakes. Evelyn then sat next to Edna as Edward stood with Carlos in the aisle and talked. Edward began, "I was eager to be back tonight and have prayer. We will go and have dinner out after tonight's prayer meeting. They were glad when I said 'Let's go!'"

Eddy-Boy, excited to see them both, looked at Evelyn and said, "Evelyn, you are really good at the piano. I been doing some writing in my spare time, songs I'd like to sing. Do you think you could help me?"

Edward and Carlos' heads turned and looked back at Eddy-Boy, surprised at his enthusiasm and at his new cultivating gift revelation. Their heads then turned to Evelyn in surprise for her response.

Feeling now that she was on the spot, Evelyn carefully responded, "Thank you, Eddy-Boy, it took me years of dedication and practice. I do love playing. I would be glad to work with you and help you, but I will tell you like my piano instructor told me, 'Don't expect me to keep feeling like this if you suddenly decide to not show up or work hard at it!'"

Eddy-Boy took a second to comprehend Evelyn's seriousness, then he said, "Now I know God is giving me the right help. I will work hard and stay disciplined."

Edna reinforced the thought by telling Eddy-Boy, "Discipline will make all your work pleasing to the Lord!"

"All right," Carlos interrupted. "I'm glad you all are here early with us, I must go and speak with Pastor Angelo. You all can discuss the details with each other, and I'll be back after my meeting." Carlos turned and walked away, leaving Edna and Evelyn discussing with Eddy-Boy the necessary details and times as Edward just looked on.

As Carlos turned to the hallway of Pastor Angelo's office, he noticed that the door was open, so he approached and went in. Pastor Angelo was seated behind his desk with his back turned, looking upon a global map with his mind deep in thought. Carlos interrupted him. "Pastor Angelo, what are you thinking about?"

Turning to look at who was there and surprised he wasn't alone in his office, Pastor Angelo then spoke up, "Oh, Carlos, glad it's you. I was just thinking of you." Pastor Angelo then turned and pulled his seat with him back to his desk. After adjusting himself, he waved and pointed to invite Carlos to have a seat. As Carlos went and took a seat, Pastor Angelo then continued saying, "I was just noticing on the map all over the world that there are people with different races, different cultures, and different languages. God knows every one of them."

"Yeah, Pastor! I know this. But what has that to do with me?" Carlos curiously asked.

At that response, Pastor Angelo then raised his head and sternly looked at Carlos and said, "Some time ago, when your father was still with us, he came in my office and sat where you are sitting. He began telling me many things, but the first thing was that he was in prayer and the Lord had revealed to him many things. One of the things he told me was that you would come in my office one day, sit where he sat, and tell me to be ready for revival. It was an amazing moment that I'll never forget. He said it with such conviction!"

Carlos looked back at Pastor Angelo with surprise and shock.

Pastor Angelo thought he upset Carlos, so he began to apologize. "I'm sorry, Carlos, and I didn't mean to offend you. You just caught me in the middle of remembering a former moment I had in this office. Forgive me now and tell me why you are here. What can I do for you?"

Carlos adjusted himself in his chair, looking right back at the pastor and said, "I'm here because I wanted to tell you that I was just in prayer at home, Evelyn and I both surrendered our wills to God and renewed our commitment to the Lord, trusting Him for everything.

He made us aware, which is why I'm here, that we been praying and asking, but now we must prepare to receive. God is bringing revival!"

Carlos' words struck Pastor Angelo like a wake-up slap. He shook his face and sat erect in his chair.

"Then God is notifying us on time. I will make the necessary announcement at tonight's service. The church board and I have already discussed you needing to be helped and encouraged to enter the ministry. Carlos, you must begin doing the work of an evangelist. You have God-given leadership skill, and I will need you to help me manage our teachers and staff. I will also personally show you and help you learn how to pastor the flock of God. Are you willing?" Pastor Angelo asked.

Carlos shook his head with a positive nod and said, "Yes." Realizing this was all being shaped and prepared by the hand of the Lord.

"Carlos, one more thing," Pastor Angelo added. "You need to start getting used to preaching and public speaking. To help you with this, I need you to be prepared every Sunday for what we will call a faith message. I want it to be five minutes or less, but I want it to be impactful, upbuilding, encouraging, even sometimes warning, but as God's messenger, delivering faithfully what He has given you to share. As a matter of fact, you have your Bible with you. Be prepared to share tonight. Can you do that?"

"I believe I can. God has been uttering this verse in my heart all day, and I been meditating on it," Carlos resolutely responded.

"That's the spirit!" Pastor Angelo shouted. "A holy messenger gives what was received from the Lord. Let's go and get tonight's meeting started. We will go and personally greet all that attend tonight, but when it is time to start our service tonight, I want you to come and sit with me on the platform. This you will do from now on, unless you are given another assignment. Understood?"

"Understood. Let's go and help every willing heart tonight be prepared for what God wants to do. Tonight we can pray and prepare, trusting God." Carlos finished saying as Pastor Angelo wrapped his arm around him and led him out the door.

Returning to the sanctuary, Pastor Angelo and Carlos split up and began greeting all who attended. There was an enthusiasm that was apparent by all that attended. They were all happy to be in the house of God that evening. It was evident by the handshakes and hugs, smiles, and high-fives. Even the Thomases were back from their vacation and in attendance. They were informed about last Sunday's service and Carlos' involvement with the youth and children's ministries. They thanked Carlos too because he gave the young people hope that they also can be useful to the Lord and His church.

Pastor Angelo made sure he spoke to and informed all the board members of his new arrangement and policy with Carlos. They were all excited for Carlos, having witnessed his growth and remembering his father, Juan Felipé, who was such an outstanding church member and believer; they were looking forward to seeing him accomplish great things for God.

Carlos was getting back to Evelyn, who was still seated with the Boyces, telling her he was going to start sitting on the platform with Pastor Angelo. As he just finished telling her, Pastor Angelo arrived behind him saying, "Let's go!" As Carlos turned to follow, Pastor Angelo waited to place his arm around Carlos and walked with him to the stage, saying to him, "Just like in the military, you have a way to do everything, same in ministry. When sitting up here, you will sit comfortably, backed into your seat, erect, and with your legs crossed, knee over knee. Understand?"

Carlos listened, looking ahead, then humbly answered, "Yes, Pastor."

This pleased Pastor Angelo, who watched as Carlos took his seat and sat appropriately. "Thank you, Carlos." He realized that Carlos knew how to follow an order and obey instruction. Pastor Angelo turned and approached the pulpit, turned on the microphone, tapped it, and drew everyone's attention. "Good evening, everyone! I want to begin tonight with some very important announcements. The first to touch on is we will not be separating today, but instead, we will all stay assembled here for prayer in the sanctuary. All will be asked to participate, including the youth and children. God hears their prayers also!

"Second, I mentioned at the conclusion of Sunday's service that we were experiencing the start of a revival with the reunification of the Boyce family, praise God, but through several confirming circumstances from the Lord, I believe it's time for us to prepare ourselves and live every day with expectation that God is going to do something entirely marvelous, beyond what we have asked or thought! So within our prayer meeting tonight, we will also be discussing what each of us can be doing as we hone our hearing to His voice and respond in obedience. We must be ready for growth and prepared to minister to the needs of new believers.

"Lastly, this stranger sitting behind me…" Everyone began laughing in the pews, they all knew he spoke of Carlos. "We all remember his father, Juan Felipé. Well, he may have departed us, but his prayers have brought us his son Carlos…of which I'm thankful! Carlos and I will be working together, with him being my ministerial intern. Remember to pray for him. I will have him doing the work of an evangelist. Tonight he will be bringing to us his first of his weekly 'faith messages.' So without further ado, I present to you Carlos DeLeon with tonight's 'faith message,' Carlos."

Carlos' first 'faith message.'

Carlos was caught in the middle of thinking about his father at the mention of his name, but he considered the moment and why he was there and arose to the pulpit. He slowly opened his Bible and laid it open at his text. Carlos looked up at his audience and grabbed his microphone and began to speak, surprising Pastor Angelo at his ability to immediately engage his audience. "Tonight's reading will be from 2 Chronicles 7:14, which we will read in a moment. I have a rhetorical question to ask of all of you, which means you don't have to answer, but let me ask you anyway. What time is it? Our text tells us the exact time you can set your watch to. I'm not talking about your fancy smartwatch, cellphone, or whatever device you use to tell your time. As the saints of God, we are supposed to be familiar with the times and the seasons, right pastor, just like the scripture testifies about the sons of the tribe of Issachar when the time came to make David king over all of Israel. Let's read our text, and I will show you how to set your spiritual clock. It will be your personal responsibility to keep it set on the right time. It tells us how. I will read this from the King James Version. Here we go.

"'If My people, which are called by My name, shall humble themselves, and pray, and seek My face, and turn from their wicked ways; *then* will I hear from Heaven, and will forgive their sin, and will heal their land.'

"Did you see it, Christian? Did you set your clock? It's right there in the middle of the verse. This is how you line up with God's timing! I'm going to have to print this up on a t-shirt, so people can ask me what it means and I can tell them. It's the word *then*, it's *then time*! When you have humbled yourself and prayed and sought His face and turned away from all of your wicked thoughts, and words, and actions, *then*!

"Who wants to go around like me and testify about the joy of being forgiven and having their conscience cleansed? You know what God does after that because He's not finished, He heals your land. That means He gets personally involved in your life right where you live because you represent Him. We will encounter people from all walks of life. Many that come will be dealing with addiction, others will be weighed with guilt and shame from sexual sin or a variety of other carnal actions like stealing, being greedy, or having terrible attitudes. Such were some of us, but we have been washed, sanctified, even justified in the name of the Lord Jesus and in the Spirit of our God.[11] So display the transformative work of our Lord Jesus with open gratefulness. Don't be ashamed to stand out and excel for you are highly favored by Him. This is what our Lord Jesus wants: He wants us to excel at all we do and whatever we are doing to humbly use it in service to Him.

"Now, we have been in prayer continuously for revival, and we will continue to stay in prayer, but God has made us aware that he is ready to start moving among His people restoring, reviving, and healing again. As we pray tonight, I want you to consider all of your hobbies and habits and prayerfully consider and ask God how to use them for ministry. We will be discussing during prayer time tonight what each of us can be doing to help. As God brings in those seeking him, it's always impressive to see the gifts of the Spirit[12] operating in the service, but to make a lasting impact, let them behold the Spirit's fruit in your life, there they will witness the power of a crucified life."[13] Carlos gathered his Bible on the pulpit then gripped it. Recognizing his pause, he stooped back toward the microphone and said, "Pastor."

Pastor Angelo was thoroughly impressed with Carlos' "faith message," but he wanted to continue with the evening's schedule of events so he approached the microphone and continued moderating. "Thank you, Carlos, for your timely message. How appropriate that was to lead us into our evening's prayer meeting. Okay, so now, if we can all stand and come forward here before the platform. We will begin with a time of corporate prayer together in a circle here." Pastor Angelo turned to Carlos and told him, "That was an outstanding message. I want us to get together Friday evening for prayer and preparation for Sunday!" Pastor Angelo started thinking about the

---

[11] 1 Corinthians 6:9–11
[12] 1 Corinthians 12:4–11
[13] Galatians 5:22–24

many things that were told him by Juan Felipé before his departure. Things were now happening just as Juan Felipé described.

"Certainly, Pastor, I will always be available for you." Carlos spoke with hopeful excitement.

"All right, let's go pray." Pastor Angelo led Carlos with him down to the prayer circle where they joined in and began to lead in prayer.

Chapter 6

Pastor Angelo stepped out from his parsonage and headed joyously toward his car. He was filled with excitement and expectation, believing God was getting ready to do a great work through the ministry at the church he pastors. He especially was looking forward to meeting with Carlos later this evening for prayer and preparation for this Sunday's worship service. Getting into his car and starting his engine, Pastor Angelo thought to turn on his radio to the local Christian radio station to listen to encouraging music, but he caught himself needing to stay focused on his meeting with Carlos, so he removed his hand from the power button.

Engaging his transmission into drive, he drove out from his driveway and entered the street.

Having approached the stop sign at the end of his street and already being moved to intense thought over the past week's events, Pastor Angelo suddenly burst into prayer as he proceeded from his stop. "Heavenly Father, I find myself shaking my head lately in amazement as I witness what is being done in people's lives by You! I remember like it was just yesterday when Juan Felipé came to the parsonage and sat and shared with me how heartbroken he was that his son left home and joined the military because he couldn't give him what he wanted. I just told him the truth: 'You can't give him everything he wants, but God can!' I encouraged him to pray daily and ask specifically for everything his son would want. He did, and it's evident *You* abundantly supplied. Thank you, God!

"Juan Felipé was a soul-winner too! The Boyces come to every meeting now because he took the time to help them when they had car trouble along the side of the road. He helped them and then shared how the Gospel changed his life, then he invited them all to church. If I remember him for anything though God, that man was a prayer warrior. He would kneel at his pew and hide his face before service would start and pray, then he would constantly pray while I would preach. I can't even count the many times I would leave him in the church praying, with Lucita waiting for him. I wanted to tell him to stop doing this, but then I would have others telling me how my sermons would greatly impact them, and that also seeing him pressing through in prayer throughout the service would inspire them to stay more fervently focused when they would pray also. I have to admit, some Sundays, I didn't feel like I gave a powerful message and delivery. I knew then his prayers made a difference.

"Forgive me, Father, I started to think he took being prayerful to an unrealistic level. But he has taught me how wrong I was. I'm now thankful for his faithful labor of love. Despite all the pain that he kept buried deep inside of him because his son Carlos would have nothing to do with him, he remained committed to asking you to stay involved in everything concerning him. When Juan Felipé came into my office and sat down and told me that Carlos would come into my office one day and tell me, 'We are going to have a revival,' I never really believed it. I thought he was just having high hopes. But here we are, just as he said, 'My son Carlos will become a man of God.' I now have him as my ministerial intern, and I'm preparing him for full-time ministry. I never even thought about it before or even considered this, but now it is becoming apparent. I never would have been able to come to this moment of thankfulness or the privilege of witnessing your anointing on Carlos' life if you never took Juan Felipé to be with you. Gracious God, I'm so thankful to you!"

Pastor Angelo was now approaching the church; as he reached the intersecting corner where the church's sign stood, he noticed Carlos was there placing an announcement on it. Carlos had the case and letters strewn about on the lawn to install a message to the sign. Pastor Angelo pulled alongside the shoulder of the street and got out of his car to greet Carlos and see what exactly he was doing. "Hey, Carlos, what's going on here?"

Carlos finished setting up his ladder to reach the height of the sign then turned and answered Pastor Angelo, "Hi Pastor, I wanted to post an inviting message for the community to see. I came early this evening because I decided to fast, so Evelyn didn't have to prepare dinner for the both of us this evening. Plus, Edna Boyce brought her son Eddy-Boy over to my house. Evelyn agreed to work with him on developing his singing voice. The man already had been writing songs to sing. I was genuinely glad to find out that his songs were about the Lord. Then I was totally in favor of it all. Evelyn is a very disciplined person, so if he can keep up with her standards for quality practice, he will do well."

Pastor remained interested in Carlos' comments, but he was more interested in knowing Carlos' need to fast, so he said, "That is interesting Carlos, and I pray the Lord looks upon Eddy-Boy and blesses all his effort. But what has me curious is your deciding to fast. Why? For revival? We can make the announcement and have all willing to participate, so it will be a church-wide undertaking. We should go ahead and do this and…"

"That is a very supportive idea, Pastor," Carlos interjected. "And we need to call upon everyone to begin to make fasting a regular practice. Especially with what we are expecting from the Lord to do. But I studied the subject in the Scriptures. What stood out to me, it even scared me to be reminded by the Lord Jesus in Scripture, that there were certain devils He said cannot be overcome *but* by prayer and fasting.[14] I don't ever want to be caught incapable or weak before the enemy, especially if a person needs my help."

---

[14] The story is told in Matthew 17:14–21, concluding with this statement.

"Very good, Carlos," Pastor Angelo acknowledged. "Sister Maria and I will join you on this purpose. I must say, though, don't ask Evelyn to join in just yet, she will need her nourishment right now for the child that God has given you two."

"You're right, I'm thankful God has given her a healthy pregnancy." Carlos agreed. "You know what, Pastor, Evelyn and I decided to go old school and wait until delivery to find out the sex of our child. It's just something we both already agreed on." Carlos kept adjusting his ladder to get ready to climb.

Pastor Angelo looked at Carlos with a proud smile. "Sister Maria and I look forward to meeting the newest DeLeon." Changing the subject and looking up at the sign, Pastor asked, "What were you going to display on the sign?"

"I wanted to display a strong pitch that would attract and invite as well be original. How's this? 'This *is* a sign! Come in and get ready. Jesus is coming!'" Carlos said with loud emphasis. "I wanted to get to the point."

"May your words echo in their hearts as they read its message. Come inside as soon as you have it finished," Pastor Angelo said as he turned and went back to his car.

Carlos went and grabbed his letters to display on the sign and arranged them to provide emphasis like he quoted. When Carlos finished setting them, he walked out to the street, near to the intersection, to get a driver's-distance view of his sign. When he realized that the message was highly visible, Carlos lifted his voice and prayed, "Father, I pray that every soul and members in their vehicle, when they pass by this way, that they see this sign, especially if they are unsaved and lost, may their hearts be moved to consider their relationship with you, and that your Holy Spirit would compel them to come and visit with us this Sunday. I pray that we are able to provide an atmosphere for faith and trust so that they can open their lives before you for salvation and healing. In Jesus's name, I pray. Amen."

After the miscellaneous letters that were strewn about were collected and placed back in their case, Carlos headed back into the church. Going back to the office area to return the case with the letters, Carlos expected to see Pastor Angelo in his office, but he wasn't there. Heading down the hallway and calling for the pastor, Carlos received no response till he entered the platform area of the sanctuary where Pastor Angelo stood before the platform, at the prayer altars, where people come to respond in prayer to God.

Pastor Angelo then spoke out to Carlos. "Right here, this is where many souls will be making their decisions for Jesus Christ. We will meet right here for this evening."

Carlos then walked forward to the front of the platform and joined Pastor Angelo.

"That is quite a bold statement you are displaying on our announcement board out there." Pastor Angelo observed. "But I like it, Carlos!"

"I wanted it to be bold and in the face. When I think about our times, it looks like the devil is throwing everything in people's faces. So I figured, now that I have a person's attention, and you see what is happening all around you, come in and get ready for the Lord's imminent return. I asked the Holy Spirit to speak to every heart that sees it," Carlos informed Pastor Angelo. "As I see it, Pastor Angelo, despite the world being in a state of utter turmoil, the power and authority of our Resurrected Lord cannot be stopped, He will come for every faithful heart that trusts in Him! These devils are all acting out because they are desperate, knowing that their time now is very short."

"You're right," Pastor Angelo acknowledged. "*But* we can't waste our time worrying about what they've done or will do. We are gathered here today to pray and prepare for what our Lord Jesus Christ will be doing. I don't believe it will just be exclusively with us, but also with His Church throughout the Earth. Carlos, I want you to come here. In our work for preparation, I want to anoint you, in obedience to the Lord, for the work He has for you." Pastor Angelo walked to the pulpit, reached inside, and pulled out a vial containing olive oil, then returned to Carlos who stood waiting for him. "As my ministerial intern, it is my responsibility to train you and make you familiar with all the various aspects of pastoral ministry, and this will be mostly done in the doing of it. But what I'm doing now is ceremonially anointing you, for the Lord has chosen you for the work He will lead you into."

Pastor Angelo then took his vial and removed the vial's cap. Looking at Carlos, Pastor Angelo asked him, "Would you take off your right shoe and sock *now?*"

Carlos, with a surprised look, nodded and then complied quickly, standing and waiting and then raising his hands over his shoulders.

"In accordance to scriptural tradition, and in acknowledgment of the truth of God's Word, which states, 'That He hath made us kings and priests unto God and His Father; to Him be glory and dominion for ever and ever. Amen.'[15] I anoint you, Carlos DeLeon, in the name of the Father, in the name of the Son, and in the name of the Holy Spirit, unto the work of His ministry. May all of your service and labor of love be done with integrity and patience, to His praise, His honor, and His glory!" Pastor Angelo takes his vial and

---

[15] Revelation 1:6 (KJV, cf. Leviticus 8:22–24, 1 Samuel 16:12–13)

begins to pour oil upon the head of Carlos. Then he pours some oil in his right hand and begins rubbing it in his hand as he walks about Carlos. When behind him, he rubs some on the lobe of his right ear then upon his right thumb. Then walks about to the front of him and places oil on his right big toe. After capping the vial and placing it down, Pastor Angelo returns to address Carlos. "May the Holy Spirit rest upon you mightily, giving you a discerning spirit and an understanding heart, to empower you to succeed in all you are led to do by Him. Don't be distracted by the words of people, or by the possessions you own, but remember 'You shall follow the Lord your God and fear Him; and you shall keep His commandments, listen to His voice, serve Him, and cling to Him!'"[16]

Pastor Angelo began praising God and worshipping in an unknown tongue as he paced back and forth before the platform. Carlos was still standing at first with his arms raised till the reality of the attention of heaven overwhelmed him, causing his chin to sink into his chest, moving him to fall prostrate on the floor, praising and thanking God.

"Father," Carlos cried, "I worship you with all of my heart! I humbly thank you for choosing me to serve you amongst the people you have redeemed unto Yourself. I must confess to You Lord that I am entirely unworthy of this, for I have been guilty of stubbornness; and I was filled with pride, thinking I could do better than my father in life, but now he is gone. Lord Jesus, I will follow you with utmost reverence, I will obey your commandments, listen to your voice, and willingly serve you. I will also cling to you closely so I may always succeed in life because, Lord Jesus, I need you!" Carlos began strongly weeping in brokenness as he continued to worship the Lord.

Pastor Angelo had paused his praying to hear Carlos' confession and dedication. He grabbed some available tissues to give to Carlos and helped him up. He escorted Carlos to one of the front pews and began to talk with him, saying, "Carlos, I'm sure you never thought about it before, and I just had recently come to realize that God has

---

[16] Deuteronomy 13:4

been actively shaping the events here at the church as well as in your life," Pastor Angelo began pointing out.

"I have been aware that God has been showing me favor and opening up opportunity for me," acknowledged Carlos.

Pastor continued, "You know, Carlos, God just recently caused me to realize that many of the recent events we have experienced were prayed for by your father and claimed by him to surely come to pass. He declared that a revival was coming, and that it would be including you. I see the hands of God moving in our services, and his powerful anointing upon you. So this begs me to ask you a question, and before I ask, I want to explain to you what I was doing when you saw me looking at the map on my wall. When you came into my office and caught me thinking while staring at a map on my wall, this was because your father, Juan Felipé, told me that you would be reaching the world with the Gospel during this revival. I was noticing that there were so many different cultures and languages, I was wondering how it could ever be done even in our lifetime. So here's the question, Carlos. What do you see happening during this revival?"

"Pastor Angelo," Carlos surprisingly responded, "I don't have a clue as to how the Lord wills this to be accomplished nor how the Lord Jesus will get it done. All I do know is from the Word of God, the precedents set by the church written in the Book of Acts. There it shows us that the priority from the beginning is Jesus. His life, death and burial, and resurrection from the grave was the subject of every sermon. The result of which was genuine repentance and a passion for prayer for their personal needs and sincere prayer for the care of their neighbor. They hungered for the Word of God and was deeply moved for everyone to know the risen Lord Jesus. Meanwhile, the Holy Spirit manifested His presence and would call people to be separated for ministry and missions work. There was even more generous giving during such a time. The people wanted to gather corporately every day for worship, prayer, and fellowship, continuing in the sacrament of the breaking of bread. The Scripture also specifically notes that they were experiencing great favor from all the people. This is what should be expected at any outpouring of revival from the Lord. Now as far as reaching the entire world with the Gospel, I can only start with what we know is helping all partic-ipating ministries now and start there. Pastor, we can start recording your messages and post them on all social media outlets. We can ask everyone who have accounts who are willing to repost the messages to hopefully help start broadening your reach and impact."

Pastor Angelo looked at Carlos like he was lost in the conversa-tion and said, "I know very little about what you are talking about, Carlos. I don't spend any time on social media. I think we should also post your 'faith message' as well for those that have a shorter attention span and aren't willing to listen to a full sermon message."

"Sure, Pastor, I'll do that, but what I'm now trying to wrap my head around is how we can get our recorded messages seen and heard by everyone?!" Carlos sat with a bewildered look on his face, realizing there was much work to be done.

"God will lead and direct you, Carlos. Don't make it harder than it already is. Pay attention to Him!" Pastor instructed.

Carlos shook his head in agreement with Pastor Angelo, realiz-ing he was just starting his work of ministry for the Lord. Carlos then began to tell Pastor Angelo the rest of his plan to help in preparation for Sunday's service. "In addition to setting up the sign, I wanted to tell you that I wanted to call and gather as many as are willing tomorrow and take them with me to knock on all the doors of the homes in the community and invite them to church. Let them get to know us and allow us to get to know them. Maybe we can help them. At the very least, we can let them all know we are willing to reach out to help."

"That is excellent, Carlos! I do want to remind you though to make time for prayer and study for your 'faith message.' I want them to be 'hot' every time," Pastor insisted. "Let's pray together now and then we'll depart. You need to get your rest."

"Okay, Pastor." Carlos smiled as he and Pastor Angelo knelt over their pew.

Pastor Angelo placed his hand on Carlos' back and began pray-ing, "Heavenly Father, we glorify and humbly worship you tonight for all that you have revealed and confirmed to us, but even more, for Who You are. You are the great King, and we submit ourselves unto you to do your will. I pray, Father, that you would bring unto Carlos all the people and resources he will need to accomplish your will. Enable me also, by your magnificent grace, to prepare Carlos also for pastoral leadership and ministry. May he be among your noted saints, faithful in his commission and to his calling."

Carlos concluded the prayer by saying, "Father, we worship you with the strength of our lives. We pray that the lives you give unto us to Shepherd would be nurtured and faithfully discipled with the Gospel we have received from You and Your apostles. May we be prepared to welcome you when you return and appear to us...and be found *faithful*! To Your honor and praise and great glory. Amen!"

Pastor Angelo and Carlos walked through the church, making sure all rooms were readied and presentable for service on Sunday. As they departed and locked the door, Pastor Angelo informed Carlos, "I've called and informed all of our staff on Sunday to arrive an hour early to meet with you. There you will be able to share any and all information and updates, have a time of prayer, and address any issues any are facing. You will now be the go-to person for anything of importance happening here at the church. Any matters that you are unable to handle bring to me promptly, and I'll address them as soon as possible." Pastor Angelo arrived at his car, entered, started the engine, and rolled down his passenger window to continue speaking to Carlos.

Carlos stepped up to the window and commented, "I get it! You want me to take up my role as the under-shepherd and take care of all the details. Very well, Pastor, I will work hard to help make your life easier."

"Thank you, Carlos," Pastor uttered with deep sincerity.

"Look, Pastor," Carlos affirmed, "you need to start taking life a little more comfortably. Do you ever listen to your radio?"

"Sometimes, but only Christian radio or the news," Pastor Angelo pointed out.

"I turn it on, and the Lord blesses me with encouraging songs every time! Try it out," Carlos suggested.

"All right," Pastor said as he reached for the power button and pressed it. Just then, a song began playing from its start: "No

Weapon" by Fred Hammond. Pastor Angelo began nodding his head to the song's rhythm and turned the volume up, put the car in Drive, and took off, with the melody drifting out the window and slowly fading from Carlos' hearing as he drove away.

Carlos kept watching, realizing the truth of the words sung.

Chapter 7

Carlos and Evelyn were sleeping soundly in bed alongside each other in the early dawn of Sunday morning when the alarm that was set by Carlos on his phone began sounding off. Carlos sat up quickly in bed, looking cautiously at Evelyn while reaching for his phone to silence it from ringing its tone. He was certainly trying to awaken early and not disturb her in doing it. Attempting to quietly roll out of bed, Evelyn rolled over toward him and said with her eyes still closed, "What are you trying to do this early in the morning? The sun is just starting to come up." Her eyes opened enough to glance toward their window.

"I'm sorry, Evelyn." Carlos reached over to her and began softly rubbing her side. "I didn't want to wake you, but I wanted to start this day early in prayer."

"Okay…but did you get your 'faith message' ready?" Evelyn said, trying to get comfortable in bed again.

Carlos began to arise and stand before he responded, "Yes, it's ready. The Lord impressed upon me a strong topic to share. I was kept up last night doing research and studying languages and their translations. I was also looking up the different methods used to share the Gospel these days. More and more, the most effective method reaching the masses now is digitally, but the same problem still exists since the time of Babel. We still don't understand one another's language."

Evelyn found her comfortable position and said to Carlos before falling back to sleep. "All right Carlos." Evelyn released a very tired yawn and finished her thought, "You'll figure it out. If not, you'll find the right people to make it happen. It's what you've done in business, coordinate this for Jesus." Having said this, Evelyn's head relaxed against her pillow, falling back to sleep.

Hearing Evelyn's response made Carlos pause and just consider her words. He nodded his head in agreement with her, realizing she's right. Carlos made his way over to his den. Upon arriving, Carlos opened up the blinds to his window, noticing that the sun had not yet fully risen upon the day. Carlos placed his slippers by his door and walked back barefoot to the window, where he knelt down and began to pray. "Holy Father, I come to you in the name of Jesus. I worship you today with outstretched arms for the 'open door' of opportunity to serve. As you know, yesterday, I went through the community around the church with some of our young people, Eddy-Boy and Donna and Ralph and Nancy. I paired them off in teams to cover each side of a street. They really did an outstanding job in witnessing and testifying the Gospel and giving personal invitation to our worship service today. I believe it to be the start of great friendships. I pray, Father, that you would establish them as witnesses, testifying of your goodness and grace through their given abilities. I'm so thankful they have learned to work well with each other.

"Heavenly Father, I worship you also in thankfulness for Pastor Angelo and all the staff at our church. I ask for a 'special anointing' to be placed upon each of them as they prepare and perform the duties assigned to each of them. Especially for the pastor, who has faithfully ministered Your Word and served your people. I pray his message today goes forth with penetrating power into the ears and hearts of those attending today, causing honest responses in prayer to You. May every person attending our service experience the ministry of the Holy Spirit working through your people, through the discussion and preaching of Your Word and bringing about the true evidence of revival: obedience to the commands of our Lord Jesus Christ, a sincere thankfulness and worship of you, and an overwhelming desire to do good to honor you.

"I continue to thank you for my mother, who is still with us and affirmed by many ladies in the church, bringing her joy and friendship. She never complains about anything, but I know that, like me, she sincerely misses my dad. But God, I really want to thank you, I praise and worship you for my wife Evelyn and our child she is carrying. I continue to pray over our child's life, and today I ask for You to protect my child from liars and fake friends who would try to convince my child to behave wickedly. May my child have boldness to confront and rebuke but also able and willing to forgive. Evelyn is a constant reminder to me that I am highly favored by you. I thank you for her insight and support. I pray I always display to her the sincerest of love and affection, for I deeply love her.

"Lord, this is my first Sunday serving as an interned minister, I pray I conduct myself humbly, giving proper regard for all. Be with me as I moderate the staff meeting as well as assisting Pastor Angelo during the service on the platform. Help me to be in agreement and compliant to your Holy Spirit, who always operates in decency and order. Lastly, Almighty God, I been looking into how to try and understand the difficulty of language translation, and how it would be possible to share the Gospel and make it available and understood by every language on the Earth. This is something beyond my education and experience, but I was given an insightful encouragement from Evelyn. She said to find the right people and coordinate the effort. God, I'm asking you to lead and direct me to the right people. Help me to understand where to focus my attention and take advantage of social media in this digital age, to inform everyone on the planet that God is just. You have made provision to save man from their sins if they will but repent and obey you. Father, I pray for you to restore people's lives. Heal their bodies and rebuild their families. You promise eternal life to us, and that is a tremendous bonus, but the real bonus is spending it with You. I worship You, Lord!"

Carlos became erect on his knees, holding his hands outstretched while his thoughts kept uttering praise to Almighty God as he peered upward toward heaven. Carlos rested back on his knees and continued to pray. He didn't want to forget any detail or person, so he continued bringing these matters up to the Lord. He trusted that He Who sits on the throne in heaven regarded him. When he was finished praying, then he arose. Closing his blinds and sliding into his slippers, Carlos went to his kitchen to make some coffee before making breakfast for Evelyn and himself.

Evelyn and Carlos arrived early and noticed Pastor Angelo and Sister Maria were there early as well at the church. After parking the car and going inside, they noticed Sister Maria headed to the kitchen. Evelyn followed her down there and discovered she was making initial preparation for a potluck dinner for later after service. Evelyn asked, "Why wasn't I informed to help prepare a dish for this occasion?"

Sister Maria responded, "Because of your pregnancy, I thought it best not to ask you."

"I'm pregnant, not handicapped or disabled. I would really like to help," Evelyn said as she went through the drawers and cabinets, pulling items for place settings at the tables.

Sister Maria noticed the sincerity of Evelyn and watched her as she continued trying to be useful and helpful. "I apologize. I won't do that again. I will at least inform you of everything. I didn't know if you would be willing and—"

"Sister Maria," Evelyn interrupted her, "I am always willing. I have surrendered to our Lord Jesus Christ, and if the church is doing something, I am a part of the church. Plus, I so look up to you. I would do anything for *you*." It was at that moment that Evelyn truly endeared herself to Sister Maria, who walked forward and lovingly hugged Evelyn. From then on they were always seen as close friends.

Carlos went to Pastor Angelo's office to share with him the events of Saturday. After greeting each other and was offered a seat by the pastor before his desk, Carlos shared. "I kept an open mind as I went and took our young people out yesterday to visit our local neighbors here and invite them personally to our Sunday worship service. As a team, we conducted ourselves with sincere friendliness. What was amazing to behold was when each of them had opportunity to testify and give their personal witness, they did, and every person we greeted were open then to discuss their personal need or challenges. Very few were unwilling to talk with us. I believe it was due to the fact that many of them heard about your ministry here but felt somewhat strange about coming in, even though living so close. It was providential for us to simply come and invite them. We also were letting everyone know also that we would be available to help with reasonable chores if needed. Many of them said they would come today. I'd like to post myself near our entrance before service begins to greet them when they come. I know all of them could possibly not show up, but then again, maybe all of them will!?!"

Pastor Angelo was enthusiastically pleased as he listened to Carlos. He swiveled happily in his chair as he answered Carlos, "You may see even more than just them. I received a few calls at home from people who were touched by your message left on our sign. They indicated that they were interested in coming to service. God is moving and taking advantage of every outreach we are making. I believe this is just the beginning. I'm glad the ladies planned a potluck dinner for today after church. It will give us time to personally meet those that come today. Good job, Carlos! Every effort is being taken into account and used by God."

Carlos sat listening and realizing that as hard as he thought he was working, God was working harder. He stood up and told the pastor, "I better get over and conduct our staff meeting. I want to make sure that we are prepared and ready as a team to serve the Lord today."

"Thank you, Carlos." Pastor Angelo noticed Carlos' diligence to his duty. "I am available if you need me. Otherwise, I will see you on the platform at the start of service."

Carlos assented with a nod and turned to the door and departed. Looking down at his smartwatch and seeing he had time, Carlos relaxed his shoulders and continued down the hallway to the stairwell leading to downstairs where he would meet with the church staff and teachers of Sunday school. As he passed the kitchen and saw Sister Maria and Evelyn busy there, they looked over at him and just pointed down toward the classroom where the others were gathered and continued working. He went inside the classroom and took the available chair at the table they were all seated at.

"Good morning to all of you and thank you for being here. I just spoke with Pastor Angelo. He confirmed that we should be seeing new people attending today, and we will welcome them. Please announce, when appropriate, that we'll be having a potluck dinner after service today, and all are invited. Hopefully they all can stay. Now, I'm sure Pastor Angelo explained and briefed you all on my role here. I want to reemphasize to all of you that I will always make myself available to all of you and provide any assistance and help you need, the Thomas's can attest to this, so please keep me informed of any and all needs ASAP. We are a team here in cooperation with the Holy Spirit to equip the saints. This is but one of our responsibilities, so to succeed in all of them, we will need continuous support and cooperation from each other." Everyone was pleased hearing Carlos' sincere straightforwardness. They also appreciated his gentle tone coupled with seriousness. Carlos was aware of the big picture and wanted each of them to know he was not going to overlook any details. So he continued. "Our responsibility is great and our duties many, we must be students and teachers, preachers and prayer warriors, all requiring from us the utmost effort. But God will honor our efforts, our labor is not vain in the Lord. I have a personal duty weighing on me that I will share with you all that I'm trying to find a solution to how to be able to have access to all the languages of the planet to translate scripture to, so the gospel has access to all the world."

Just then, everyone spoke their comments, but the noise was overcome by Brother Thomas, who spoke clearly and over everyone else, "You know what might help you start? We have some young people here that are serious computer nerds. They might help you in your quest. Share with them your ideas."

Carlos got excited at the news but resisted showing it, "Who in particular should I talk to?"

"Ralph, most definitely," Cathy Winters, the church's secretary said without hesitation. "He set up our system here at the church."

"Thank you, Cathy, that is where I'll start this quest then." Carlos pulled himself back to the table and resumed the meeting. "I'm sure we are all prepared for today's lessons to teach, but we all are lacking one thing before we embark on today's mission: communal prayer. Let's lift each other up now in prayer so that our efforts are surrounded by divine support and agreed petition. Let us pray..." Carlos led as they all prayed together for one another for this day's events. He then concluded and dismissed the meeting, personally encouraging them all very warmly.

As he left the classroom and walked back toward the kitchen where Evelyn and Sister Maria were, Evelyn spoke up as he entered without even looking at Carlos. "Did you grab your video camera and set it up already?" Evelyn said as she continued working.

Carlos was stopped dead in his tracks. "I forgot to bring it in. I'll go get it now." So he then makes an about face, and Carlos was off to get the video camera and its tripod from his car.

As Carlos was pulling out his tripod and bag from his car trunk, alongside him passed Ralph on his neat-looking e-bike. Ralph was locking up his bike to its parking rack when Carlos caught up to him and got his attention. "Hey, Ralph, great work yesterday. I'm expecting to see some of the people we witnessed to and invited for service to show today. I have something I want to talk to you about." Carlos began his inquiry, but Ralph kept looking at what was in his hands and responded.

"I know, you want me to set up and run the camera during the service now," Ralph said as he continued to remove and secure all his gear in his backpack.

Carlos didn't expect that response from him but agreed to the idea, saying, "Well…okay. But I wanted to ask you something along a different subject. I was just going to set up the camera and start it at the start of service."

"Bad idea. Someone needs to be present at the camera at all times to ensure things are working as they should. Can I see what you have?" Ralph reached for Carlos' bag, looked inside, and saw a Canon EOS R5 camera. "Is this your personal camera? This is the finest available for personal use. Wow, you got a wide angle and telephoto lens too! Nice gear. I'll take good care of it. I have editing software and apps at home on my computer. I can make them look professionally done." Ralph then went looking into the bags' pockets, noticing additional accessories.

Carlos was surprised at Ralph's interest in his camera, but he wanted to get to his original question. "I'm very glad for your help with this, but what I wanted to ask you about was if you could help me find a solution to biblical translation to all the world's languages."

Ralph looked up from peering into the camera bag at Carlos. "I am an electronics geek and a gamer. I'm even pretty good at writing code, even algorithms, but when you're dealing with language, you have a lot of variables that can't be handled by a computer. I'll take a look at it when I get home later."

"Thank you, Ralph," Carlos was relieved to know he is going in the right direction for answers. "We can meet later in the week to discuss this further. Let's go set the camera up."

Ralph closed the bag up and told Carlos, "I got it! If there is anything else I need, I will ask Ms. Williams." Ralph slung the bag over his shoulder and grabbed the tripod from Carlos and went into the church.

Carlos looked at him going in for a second then turned around and glanced heavenward and said, "Thanks, God." When his eyes came down and he looked around, he noticed the parking lot was filling up. Carlos stayed where he was to greet all the attendees as they approached the entrance. He warmly greeted all as they came in and pointed out to those that were arriving for the first time where to go for Sunday school prior to the morning's worship service later that morning.

As everyone went inside to their designated classrooms for Sunday school, Carlos thought it to be a good idea to continue to walk throughout the church while praying. He thought to himself, *If Dad can pray for the pastor all throughout the worship service, I'll pray for our teachers throughout their time in Sunday school.* When the worship service time drew near, Carlos went and stood in the vestibule to welcome any others coming to participate in worship. While standing there and the classrooms dismissed, everyone all went and gathered in the sanctuary. When the teachers came along and brought up the rear, several of them stepped out to the vestibule to tell Carlos their experience.

"Carlos, there was a mighty presence of God today in my class," Sister Thomas emphasized.

"The teens today were showing an incredible hunger for the Word of God," Brother Thomas pointed out.

Sister Anna stepped up to Carlos and said to him, "Oh, I had such a time sharing about the kindness of God today with the children. They were demonstrating it to each other afterward."

Carlos looked at her and said to her, "Thank you for your gentleness with the little ones." Looking toward the door and seeing no one else approaching the entrance, Carlos turned and told them, "Let's go worship!"

Carlos made his way up unto the platform and sat next to Pastor Angelo. As he got comfortable in his seat, he began to gaze upon all the congregants with Pastor Angelo. They were noticing all the gladness displayed by everyone, happy to be present in church that morning.

Carlos leaned toward Pastor Angelo and told him, "Good things have been happening all morning!"

Pastor raised his eyebrows with an enthusiastic smile and said, "The presence of God is evident here today. I'm going to start this service!" Pastor Angelo approached the pulpit and greeted everyone, introducing himself and Carlos as his ministerial intern and associate. He then reminded everyone of the potluck dinner that would follow the worship service and asked for all to stay. Pastor thought that it was best to take the offering early as well, so he did. He wanted to get it out of the way and not let it interrupt the flow of the service. After the offering detail was done, Pastor Angelo returned to the pulpit and grabbed the microphone. Sister Maria had just arrived and took her seat behind the piano, so he addressed the church. "Let's welcome the Lord Jesus Christ into our presence this morning with a song." He then took the lead and began singing and Sister Maria joined in on the piano…

> We have come into His House
> And gathered in His name
> To Worship Him
> (Repeat)
> We have come into this house
> And gathered in His Name
> To worship Christ the Lord
> Worship Him, Christ the Lord.[17]

Pastor Angelo had them sing it one more time, leading them through all of its verses, then he asked them all to grab their hymnals resting on the back of each pew and turn to "I'll Fly Away."[18] As they reached for their hymnals, he declared, "Some of you are ready to go, but today, all of us can be prepared to ever be with the Lord. Stand up and sing with me."

Everybody sang and was peering over each other's shared hymnals to join in the verses, for the pews were full. Children went and ran down the aisles with their arms spanned while they traveled, joining in the chorus. People swayed and raised their hands as the unity of worship was displayed. When the song concluded, many were shaking hands and complimenting each other's singing as they returned to their seats.

---

[17] Popular Church Hymn, written in 1976 by Bruce Ballinger.
[18] Popular Church Hymn, written in 1929 by Albert E. Brumley.

Pastor Angelo, witnessing all the unified fellowship, mounted the microphone and addressed the churchgoers, "I want to move this meeting along in obedience to the Spirit of God. You're now ready for the Word of God today. To begin with, we are going to boost your spirit today with a faith message, presented by my associate minister, Carlos DeLeon. Carlos."

Carlos preaches a reviving 'Faith Message.'

Carlos stepped to the pulpit and set his Bible down and opened it to his text. He then went and grabbed the microphone and greeted everyone, "Good morning, nice to see all of your happy faces today at worship. God impressed upon me a verse to share with you, it's found in 1 John chapter 5. That's the fifth book from the back of your Bible. While you're turning there, I'll share a comment, then we'll read. Now, nobody wants to be recognized as a loser. I realize that many of you are struggling and trying to cope with the cost of living and even life itself. Today we are going to listen to an apostle named John who walked with Jesus. He wanted to keep things simple and easy in his letter. In fact, he's going to tell us how to be a winner. I'll be reading from the New Living Translation to keep the English simple, and we'll look at the original Greek too.

> Everyone who believes that Jesus is the Christ has become a child of God. And everyone who loves the Father, loves his children too.
> We know we love God's children if we love God and obey his commandments.
> Loving God means keeping his commandments, and his commandments are not burdensome. (1 John 5:1–3)

"Here is the verse I want us to focus on, verse 4, 'For every child of God defeats this evil world, and we achieve this victory through our faith!' Wait one. What? Huh? Our 'faith'? What's that mean? Let's look at the original Greek and see exactly what the apostle John meant. The word John uses is the word *pistis*, which is from the root form of the word *peitho*. That word means to be persuaded of what is trustworthy. Have you been totally convinced yet? Are you confident in what you believe? Are you yet persuaded that these holy scriptures are for real? Then don't be ashamed to tell it or hesitant to obey it! God and his Word are trustworthy. If you have become confident and are persuaded that Jesus is God's Son, and that his Word is worthy of being obeyed. Then you will be showing genuine love to God and to your neighbor. Those that do are already now declared a winner in life and over this world. Living your life as a God-declared winner you won't have troubles and confusion about your sexuality or gender. You won't need a drug just to get you through your day. You won't have to steal to think that's how you can make ends meet. You'll be convinced, persuaded, and have confidence that in *all* things God…*is*…*able*! You will then know that you are ready to stand with all the saints when he returns, and 'fly away.'" Carlos made a whirling turn with his arms spread wide like the children did during worship then concluded, "This is the 'blessed hope' for those that believe!"

Carlos grabbed his Bible and went to his seat on the platform. Pastor Angelo arose with his Bible and notes and was placing them on the pulpit when an attendee stood up and addressed the pastor.

"Pastor, I'm not wanting to be rude, but I wanted to ask you a question."

Pastor Angelo continued setting his notes down and opened his Bible while responding with a calm and welcoming demeanor, "Sure, go ahead and ask me. I'm still getting my material ready."

"Pastor, I'm a backslider. While I listened to that young man preach, my heart ached within me to come forward and pray! Can I come forward to pray?" the visiting congregant pleaded.

Pastor Angelo leaned into the microphone to answer the gentleman, as he began to reply a woman stood up and interjected, "Pastor, I want to pray too. And I want my two children to come along. I want us to be ready!" The woman grabbed her children and went to the prayer altars before the platform and began to pray.

Suddenly, people from all over the congregation arose and approached the prayer altars till they were filled. People came and began standing behind them, loudly praying and confessing their need before God at the front of the church. Pastor Angelo began signaling women and members of the church board to assist people in prayer.

People fill the prayer altars.

Pastor Angelo turned to Carlos, who immediately approached him with an amazed look and admitted to him, "Looks like God Almighty made the altar call today. Let's go minister to the sheep." Pastor Angelo and Carlos went through and prayed with every person at the altar, praying for needs and witnessing others confessing repentance and accepting Jesus Christ as their Savior and Lord. Great joy was shared and many tears flowed, for they were happy to be a part of the family of God.

As soon as the attendees were cleared from the prayer altars, the potluck dinner was announced and all stayed. The potluck meal was a great time of fellowship. Sister Maria was pleased enough food was available to feed all that attended. Pastor Angelo encouraged her by reminding her, "God always knows exactly what is needed!"

Chapter 8

Pastor Angelo and Carlos made sure that everyone was spoken to and encouraged as the potluck concluded. Each were given a personal farewell before they departed. Carlos stayed with the pastor till they came alongside Ralph, who just sat down and was enjoying his full plate of food. Pastor realized that Ralph had become the new church videographer, so he looked at them both and said, "I'll leave you two to discuss the details, I need a plate of food if there is anything left!"

Carlos grabbed a chair across from Ralph and began his conversation, "Now I know you want to take what was recorded and edit it, which is great, but the idea Pastor and I have is we want it posted on social media."

Ralph was enjoying his meal but listening, "Which one in particular?"

"All of them, if we can do it," Carlos informed and enquired.

Ralph calmly responded, "I can do it. But I only have recorded your faith message today, not Pastor's sermon."

"I know, but we have to start somewhere," Carlos answered. "I want to also start staying linked to all the other churches in our city. I want to stay informed of what they are doing. If it is a helpful service or ministry, post it in our bulletins and repost online. We, as the church, cannot remain islands any longer. We have to become a strong network of holy response, always sharing the grace of God. In the near future, I want us to be able to post the latest status and need for world missions and Bible translation. This, I believe, is the mandate of the church."

Ralph saw how serious Carlos got and told him, "I'll edit your message and post it on every useful platform. I'll set up usernames and passwords for the various media and make a list of them and get them to you and Pastor Angelo. Afterward, I'll look into those translation questions you had and make a current inquiry into world missions. When do you need that information?"

Carlos was impressed with Ralph's can-do attitude and said, "Tuesday evening, I'll come by your home and meet with you. I'll call you when I'm on my way."

"Okay, Carlos, but I want to remind you," Ralph tried to speak in the middle of his chewing, "you're going to be right among the various thoughts, opinions, and mindsets of people from all around the world. People that don't agree or don't care will just scroll past it."

"I'm aware," Carlos assured Ralph. "We will pray for God to use our effort and continue to preach and teach, share what the church is doing, and network with other ministries. We must occupy with obedient efforts until He comes back."

"All right, Carlos," Ralph kept eating, and trying to talk, "I'll set up the accounts and use my skills on each site to give them a professional and inviting appearance. You can check it out when you come see me on Tuesday and let me know if everything is acceptable, then we'll roll from there."

"After I get off work on Tuesday, I'll stop and have dinner with the wife, then I'll be over. See you then," Carlos said as he arose from his chair and returned it under the table, leaving Ralph to finish his meal.

The days began going by swiftly. Tuesday came and went, and Carlos was so looking forward to dinner with his beautiful wife Evelyn that evening. As he got into his car, he called to let her know he was on his way. "Hey, Ev, on my way home for dinner with my beautiful wife. Now we can have dinner when I arrive, or we can just go and make another baby?"

Evelyn smiled at hearing his voice. She loved his not-so-subtle attempts at romance with her. "You just get home. I'm hungry and been waiting for you to arrive to eat. Besides, we haven't yet had our first baby. When we do, I pray God gives us some time to just practice. I been thinking of you too, Carlos, I have a whole lot of love to give to you..."

"I like your thinking," Carlos shot back, "hurrying my behind home. See you when I see you!"

"See you when I see you," Evelyn said as she hung up and clutched her belly and smiled again, thinking of Carlos.

Evelyn took her time setting their table, and when she was finished, she sat down waiting for Carlos to arrive. Carlos pulled into the garage and exited his car as if in a ballet and sashayed inside the door. Carlos hung up his jacket with rhythmic movements then continued sashaying through the hallway till he arrived to his dining room and saw Evelyn and struck a pose. He said, "There...is my beautiful wife!" Carlos rose up, as if to stand upon his toes, then pirouetted and sashayed toward Evelyn and then embraced her from behind affectionately. Evelyn really appreciated the gestures by Carlos, even though it was not the best of form, for she was a ballerina when they first met.

Carlos' hands rubbed Evelyn's shoulders, and he continued rubbing them as they began to slide down her arms and settled upon her stomach. His hands caressed her belly as he told her, "I love my wife!" with a sincerely loving tone in her ear. He kept caressing and holding her belly and kissed her cheek. Evelyn adjusted in her chair and kissed Carlos' cheek back as he continued embracing her. Just then, the child started moving in Evelyn's womb and began kicking. Carlos was awestruck with his mouth wide open.

"The baby has been doing that a lot lately when I pray, but I think now it is responding to hearing Daddy's voice. Let's eat. I'm hungry!' Evelyn said as she straightened up in her chair.

Carlos pushed her chair into the table. "Starting today I will be welcoming you also now to our dinner table." Carlos went around and took his seat and prayed, "Heavenly Father, thank you for providing our dinner that we share in your presence. We welcome our newest addition to this family, to our table, and ask that our child may be made to understand the privilege we enjoy of your abiding presence, through Jesus Christ our Lord. Amen."

Carlos was doing most of the talking during dinner because Evelyn *was* hungry. So he continued and started sharing details occurring at work and with coworkers that Evelyn had met. She enjoyed knowing how they were doing and what was being accomplished by them. When Carlos then turned the discussion to what happened at church last Sunday, Evelyn lit up and began commenting on things she observed during the service.

"Carlos, I'm thankful to God for those that came to service Sunday and accepted Christ. With all the violence happening everywhere, it is apparent that only through Jesus Christ can all of us find real peace," Evelyn pointed out.

"This is true. Pastor and I both can only acknowledge that God is loudly calling men and women everywhere to repent and allow Him to do a transformative work in their life into the image of His son, Jesus." Carlos continued saying, "This is why I'm also working with Ralph now. We are setting up accounts on social media representing our church not only to share the Word of God but also to coordinate with other churches and ministries to help each other have a stronger reach and impact, as well as keep everyone informed of ministries and services that are available to help all who have need. In fact, I have to get ready to go see Ralph and check on how the initial setup looks."

"Get going then. I'll clean all this up." Evelyn started clearing the table to the kitchen. Meanwhile, Carlos started finishing off his plate. When she returned, Evelyn mentioned, "I'll go over a number of songs I picked up for Eddy-Boy to rehearse on to help exercise his singing range. You keep getting busier and busier, I'm going to have to do the same."

"Aw, Ev, I'm sorry if I've been too preoccupied with ministry and work and neglected you," Carlos said as he sorrowfully looked upon Evelyn.

Evelyn saw his face and reminded Carlos, "Since we surrendered to the Lord, we don't have the luxury to choose what we want to do. Right now we have the luxury of time, to serve. We both are needed for service and ministry right now. I pray, right now, that after our baby is born, that God provides for us convenient times to 'practice', even though then we both will probably be even busier."

Carlos stared at Evelyn and said with conviction, "I constantly thank God and admit that I'm blessed to have a beautiful and thoughtful wife like you. I love you, Evelyn!"

Evelyn was deeply touched by Carlos' response and it showed. Evelyn composed herself and told Carlos, "Okay, get going over to Ralph's and make sure everything is set up well. I look forward to seeing it later." Evelyn started to turn away from the table with her hands full but then turned back and caught Carlos' attention. "Carlos, I'm the one who is truly blessed. I have a husband who follows and obeys the Lord Jesus Christ. A woman can't ask for better than that."

Carlos answered, "Thank you, Evelyn, that means a lot to me." Carlos watched Evelyn return to the kitchen then did a spinning move off his seat and sashayed back out to his car.

Carlos called Ralph as he departed his garage to let him know he was on his way over. Ralph had already set up multiple social media accounts for the church, so all he had to do was go to his room and boot up his computer and wait for Carlos.

When Carlos arrived, he was excited to see Ralph because he realized this was the start of their church having a worldwide outreach. Ralph was excited to see him as well, especially because he wanted to bring him up to date on all the recent interactions and responses on social media. So Ralph led Carlos into his house and brought him into his bedroom, which impressed Carlos at his huge bedroom and its setup.

Ralph kept his room clean and organized. Carlos was certainly surprised; he remembered keeping his bedroom clean but never this organized. His gaming setup was across from his bed, so he could play from there, too, if he wanted. He had two unique gaming seats with built-in cup holders and speakers built into the head rests and an additional surround sound system for gaming or movies. As they walked by and approached his desk area, Carlos noticed that Ralph had studied how to be efficient with space and equipment. He had there a high-performance desktop computer with two additional monitors mounted above its main screen, side by side. It was connected also to his television monitor as well, giving him interconnected usability.

Carlos admired his setup and told Ralph, "Nice! Where did you learn how to do all this? This is an excellent setup. I could definitely hang out here and have a lot of fun."

"My older brother, Ryan, he's really good!" Ralph began to explain. "I've been learning from him since I was ten years old. He says he's advanced, but I say he's at expert level. I'm still at intermediate level because I need more experience time. But I have been actively writing code now for years and accomplishing things. I just need the ideas and know the needs to start a new project. Any needs, let me know, maybe I can help. Let me turn on the TV and play your faith message. Check it out."

"Very good and clear recording! You did a good job at following me on the platform with a steady focus. Thanks, Ralph," Carlos observed.

"Here, let me bring up a few of the social media accounts and put them on the monitors. I want to show you the feedback that was given on some of the sites." Ralph then began displaying them on the screens for Carlos to read.

"It looks like many of them have questions about scripture that they want answered. Some don't understand what they've heard or read. The others are just making comments about me and my looks. But looking at the media sites, their appearance looks great! Nice job," Carlos noticed.

"Yeah, the girls and some of the guys think you're hot. But I was noticing this and thought you'd be all day responding to them. Instead, what I thought would be great for you to try is to offer a podcast. You can have guests, accept callers, and just address questions that would be submitted every week. I can announce it on social media, request questions to be addressed, limit it to a subject every week, and build a direct discussion outreach every week. What do you think?" Ralph made his pitch to address the apparent need.

Carlos was thinking about it for a second then said, "We would have to gather and assemble the equipment, and then—"

Ralph then interrupted Carlos. "I already have the equipment. We just need a location that we can soundproof for good audio quality, and we'll be set and ready. I know how to do this, Carlos. I can act as the show's producer and handle the details."

"We could probably use a room at the church, right!?" Carlos thought out loud to Ralph.

"Yeah, I think that idea will work." Ralph kept offering his ideas. "I will announce this right away on the social media sites and ask for questions people want addressed. I'll tell them we will answer the three most requested with a biblical response during your podcast. Afterward, we can keep each podcast along a subjected theme to focus on. We can also report on and bring everyone up to date on the current status of world missions and Bible translation needs. I think we will be covering a lot of bases on each podcast."

Carlos shook his head in agreement. "I think we are on the right track and providing an informative service. Set it all up, and I will inform Pastor Angelo of the details and give him the usernames and passwords to these accounts. Thanks, Ralph, you're giving this a great effort, and God is blessing every effort we are giving Him."

"Okay, Carlos, we can be ready to broadcast as soon as Thursday evening. I'll put that on the announcement if it's okay with you." Ralph was getting all the details finalized. "By the way, language translation still needs human involvement. No one can write code or set up an algorithm for a language translation no one yet knows or been exposed to. However, artificial intelligence is going to be a big help to translators in the nearby future, perhaps speeding up their work.

Carlos smiled at Ralph's excitement. "Yeah, AI will be dipping its nose into everything, but as far as the podcast, let's go ahead and do it! I guess if this touches everything…I'll just get ready to go back home then."

"Wait a second." Ralph was eager to ask Carlos. "Want to play a game?"

"Thought you'd never ask." Carlos was relieved at the invitation. "Do you have Call of Duty, Modern Warfare?"

"Of course I do." Ralph went over to his PlayStation 5 and turned it on. "You ever play this game?"

Carlos went over and selected his seat and sat then grabbed his controller. "I lived it. Let's go!"

Carlos stayed for a couple more hours with Ralph playing the game. He was sharing with Ralph, while playing, many of the experiences he had while involved in actual combat. He wanted Ralph to understand that real combat was more than just point and shooting at the enemy; it was a disciplined action and coordinated effort with all soldiers performing their role with purpose.

Carlos finally realized the time and told Ralph, "I better take a thorough look at all those comments and questions that were posted on social media before I go."

"Go ahead, Carlos," Ralph answered. "I'm going to finish this game and increase my kills-to-death ratio. Don't try to count them up. I'll do the sorting, that's easy."

Carlos was at Ralph's desk scrolling through the various responses. "I know you'll have them ready and sorted. I'm looking forward to answering their questions when we do our first podcast. If it's okay with you now, I'm going to start heading home. Thanks for setting up these accounts and handling all these details. I'll see you at prayer meeting tomorrow. I'll let myself out."

As Carlos started walking to leave Ralph's room, Ralph paused his game and addressed Carlos on one more important detail.

"I need to know for the announcement on the social media sites, what are we going to call the podcast?" Ralph enquired.

Carlos stopped, turned around, and with a serious face, said, "The Church! We will call it The Church podcast. The gates of hell will not be able to overpower it!"[19]

---

[19] A reference to a quote made by the Lord Jesus Christ in Matthew 16:18.

Chapter 9

When Wednesday night came about, Carlos was excited about arriving at church early to inform Pastor Angelo of all the progress made in creating accounts on various social media sites. Pastor Angelo asked Carlos to make a detailed announcement at the start of their prayer meeting to inform the church of its newest outreach effort extended to the entire world via social media. Carlos also announced the new podcast outreach that was to be started to answer questions from a biblical point of view, share world missions and Bible translation status and needs, and announce various services and ministries that are available to those having need. Before the prayer meeting ended, Pastor Angelo had Carlos and Ralph come forward and the church prayed to God for him and Ralph and their continued effort to reach out to the world via the podcast broadcast.

As Thursday evening arrived, Carlos had already made arrangement with Evelyn to bring her to Pastor Angelo's home to be with Sister Maria. Pastor Angelo wanted to be with Carlos at the church to see how Ralph would set up the studio there. Carlos was glad Pastor Angelo would be there for his support. He even thought he would participate in the podcast, but Pastor Angelo had a wait-and-see attitude about it. He was still wondering how a "podcast" could be set up at the church and have a worldwide reach. So after arriving at the pastor's home and leaving Evelyn there with Sister Maria, Carlos and Pastor Angelo went to go pick up Ralph and all the equipment he had. Carlos didn't know how much extra room he needed so he brought Evelyn's SUV, a GMC Yukon Denali XL with the SLT trim, to ensure he had adequate space for all of it. Pastor buckled in and was looking around at the huge interior as Carlos took off. When Carlos finally turned onto the street, he told Pastor Angelo, "Oh yeah, it's nice and roomy. Evelyn has a knack for what she believes is the best, plus, she could afford it."

"This is so comfortable and big," Pastor Angelo kept observing the details of the cabin. "I feel small in here!"

Carlos kept his eyes on the road and said in response, "We may need the room. I have to call Ralph and tell him we are on our way." Carlos' phone was automatically connected to his entertainment system via Bluetooth, so he commanded, "Call Ralph." The number was instantly dialed. After a couple of rings, Ralph answered and his voice was heard clearly through the vehicle's sound system.

"Ay, Carlos, I have everything packed and ready to go. I would've left already to the church but not enough room in my car to carry all the equipment," Ralph explained.

"We're okay, Ralph, I'm on my way," Carlos replied. "I have my wife's SUV, plenty of room for all the gear. Pastor Angelo is with me. We'll be there shortly."

After easily loading all the equipment that was neatly packaged and boxed into the SUV, they headed to the church. As they took off, Ralph then apprised Pastor Angelo and Carlos of all the gear they loaded. "Okay, the equipment I have is originally intended for remote podcasting on the go, but the quality is acceptable by any standard.

The bulk of the boxes are soundproofing acoustic panels. I wanted to make sure we had enough to soundproof any space we use. Plenty of room in this vehicle to handle carrying it all. Setup should take no time at all," Ralph explained.

"Good," Carlos responded, "I also prepared my notes for announcements, which I will do at the start of the podcast following our introduction to the worldwide audience. Write down those three popular questions for me with the most popular listed last."

Ralph was right, setup was done pretty quickly, with all hands participating. An adjacent room to Pastor Angelo's office was used. It was used for minor storage and easily cleared to set up a table and chairs for the podcast. With the equipment all set up and Ralph doing a preliminary sound check, Ralph lifted three fingers to Carlos to indicate three minutes till they would go live. Carlos went quickly over all his notes and set up his phone as his clock and put it on the table in front of him.

Pastor Angelo sat at one end of the table and put on a pair of headphones to follow along with the podcast. Carlos then asked if he still wanted to be a part of the podcast. "Pastor, do you want to be on the podcast?"

Pastor Angelo had to adjust his headphones; he wasn't used to hearing Carlos' voice right into his ears. "Carlos, I am just here to witness and support what you and Ralph are doing."

"Thank you, Pastor!" Carlos understood this was his show alone, so he wisely bowed his head and prayed, "Father, thank you for this opportunity to begin an outreach to the entire world. I pray to represent the church well and its needs and available services. I ask for you to enable me to rightly divide your Holy Word clearly and with authority, to bless and help, warn and exhort all who would listen so they would know what the Creator of heaven and earth has spoken, in Jesus's name, amen."

Carlos looked up, and Ralph held up one finger. Carlos looked at his phone's clock, took a deep breath, and shook his head to show he was ready. As the time approached, Ralph lifted one hand and completed the countdown, folding in his fingers and cued Carlos with a pointed finger at him.

"Welcome to the Church podcast!"

"Welcome to The Church podcast. This is Carlos DeLeon, and I am your host. With me is my producer and jack of all electronic trade, Ralph. Thank you, Ralph. Also, my special guest for today is my pastor, Pastor Angelo Romero. He is pastor of the Church of God in our humble midwestern city of Aurora, Illinois. We have a lot to cover today, but I do have the three most requested questions concerning Holy Scripture that you have submitted to us on social media. We will get to them later in this podcast, but first, I have to announce some important information. Here we go… Now one of the purposes of this podcast, besides addressing your questions from a biblical point of view, is to inform, share, and unite with ministries and churches all over the world. That's right, the local church is now a worldwide entity, living and breathing 24-7, 365. So let me begin this by reporting a couple of ministries that this podcast fully supports. I'm sure there will be more in the future, but these first two will always be at the top because they are most important to the ministry of the Church. The first is…Church of God World Missions.

"The Church of God World Missions exists to

- preach the gospel of Jesus Christ,
- develop mature disciples for the kingdom of God,
- lead non-Christian people to salvation,
- help unchurched or nominal Christians become committed disciples of Christ,
- train national leaders to proclaim the gospel to their own people and to other nations,
- help relieve people who are suffering and in need.

"This information is taken directly from their website. Contact them at www.cogwm.org for donations and/or involvement, which is graciously appreciated, or for more information.

"The second is…illumiNations. Illuminations envisions all people of the world having access to God's Word by 2033. Goals believed to be achieved by that time are as follows:

- 95% will have access to a full Bible.
- 99.96% will have access to a New Testament.
- 100% will have access to at least some portion of Scripture.

"illumiNations hosts a collective impact alliance of Bible translation partners and resource partners working together to eradicate Bible poverty in this generation. Contributions are accepted and further information is found on their website at www.illuminations. bible. If you want to find yourself working with the Lord Jesus and His Church, don't hesitate to get involved! God promises a special reward for those that do! Okay, now, we are going to get to those questions you have submitted to us. I asked our producer, Ralph, to give them to me with the least popular being first. All right, here we are. Thank you, Ralph. The third most popular question submitted to us is, 'Why are we told to not take revenge on anyone, even if they have done us cruelly wrong?'

"Whew, what a very good question. And we have two more, better than this one. My producer, Ralph, reminds me that the other two were requested more. Okay, we will get to them, but this is an issue all of us have to come to grips with. This subject is so important the Lord Jesus himself addressed the subject, and so did the apostles. Let me read a couple of verses of Scripture to shed a bright light on this. In Leviticus 19:18, it reads, 'You shall not take vengeance, nor bear any grudge against the sons of your people, but you shall love your neighbor as yourself; I am the Lord.'[20] One more verse will really bring this home to everyone. Here it is: Romans 12:19 reads, 'Never take your own revenge, beloved, but leave room for the wrath of God, for it is written, "Vengeance is Mine, I will repay," says the Lord.'[21] These two verses really explain it well. So don't lose your love for your neighbor, love them anyway. And trust God to repay, He knows all the details, better than you do.

"What is our second question for today's podcast?" Carlos looked to Ralph then turned back toward his mic. "Thank you for that question. That was a very good one." Ralph came and handed Carlos a piece of paper. "Here it is, second most requested question, and it reads, 'Does the Bible say these are the last days, and what should we be doing?' Very good question, and thank you to all of you who seriously enquired. First, we want to confirm what the Bible says about the last days, then we'll look at what we are instructed to do.

"The Bible doesn't specifically say when are the 'last days,' but it does describe the type and behavior of people revealing this time. Also, the social and atmospheric occurrences and national conflicts will clue you in that you are approaching global tribulation and judgment. Let's read the words of the Lord Jesus Christ in Matthew 24:14, 'This gospel of the kingdom shall be preached in the whole world as a testimony to all nations, and then the end will come.'

---

[20] Scripture quotations taken from the New American Standard Bible 1995 (NASB)

[21] Ibid.

"This is why we, as the Church, forcefully promote world missions and Bible translation. This is not to rush to any judgments, but that men and women all over the world will repent and be saved! Now as for what we ought to be doing, there is a lot of instruction from the apostles, but let me exhort you with a reading from the apostle Peter in 1 Peter 4:7–11[22] where he wrote,

> The end of all things is near; therefore, be of sound judgment and sober spirit for the purpose of prayer.
>
> Above all, keep fervent in your love for one another because love covers a multitude of sins.
>
> Be hospitable to one another without complaint.
>
> As each one has received a special gift, employ it in serving one another as good stewards of the manifold grace of God.
>
> Whoever speaks, is to do so as one who is speaking the utterances of God; whoever serves is to do so as one who is serving by the strength which God supplies; so that in all things God may be glorified through Jesus Christ, to whom belongs the glory and dominion forever and ever. Amen.

"Wow! I'm excited. We're all excited here at the podcast, for we serve a great king. I'm ready for the most requested question submitted to this podcast. Let me have it, Ralph." Ralph hands him a folded note. "Thank you, Ralph. Okay now, the most popular question submitted to this podcast is, does God love the LGBTQ community, and will he accept them to heaven?'

"Well, now, we have had some very interesting questions asked already, but it appears, with this being the most popular question, that we either have many concerned for this community of people

---

[22] Ibid.

or many from this community have seen my initial 'faith message' offered on social media and are responding. Remember, we are not offering personal opinions. What we are offering is the Word of God, rightly divided, to apply to your life. We are nobody's judge. Ralph is telling me we do have a caller, our first to this podcast. Let's welcome them to The Church podcast. Caller, give us your name then tell us your question or need."

"Hello, my name is Cynthia. I actually am one of those asking your most popular question today. But I'm not even interested in your answer because the fact is, I'm a happy lesbian. I don't need a man. I don't care about your Bible, your God, or what your opinion of me is. I know you don't even care about me. I called to share my need…my need is to tell you…to go to hell!" Cynthia abruptly hangs up.

Pastor Angelo grabbed his microphone and angrily began to speak, "I have a scripture to share with you—"

Immediately, Carlos cut into Pastor Angelo's outburst and said, "Pastor, it's okay. I got this. Cynthia gave us her question, and now she called in to share her need. I see your need, Cynthia, you want honesty. You gave us your honesty, I'll give you mine."

Pastor Angelo focused his stare at Carlos as he responded.

"Cynthia, I hope you're still listening. I have a beautiful wife, who I live with in holy matrimony, who is right now pregnant with our first child. You can't say I don't care about you because even though I don't know you, I voluntarily joined the Marines. I even fought in a war. I stood on duty, pulled watches, manned patrols all to defend your rights and your freedom here to choose to do what you want. I am not here to debate anybody, argue, or look down my nose and criticize. I simply want to give you an answer from the Holy Scriptures to your question. Matter of fact, I want to read to you from the gospel of Luke 13:1–5.[23] These are words spoken by the Lord Jesus Christ.

> Now on the same occasion there were
> some present who reported to Him about the

---

[23] Ibid.

Galileans whose blood Pilate had mixed with their sacrifices.

And Jesus said to them, 'Do you suppose that these Galileans were greater sinners than all the other Galileans because they suffered this fate?

I tell you, no, but unless you repent, you will all likewise perish.

Or do you suppose that those eighteen on whom the tower of Siloam fell and killed them were worse culprits than all the men who live in Jerusalem?

I tell you, no, but unless you repent, you will all likewise perish.'"

When Carlos concluded his scriptural response, he looked up at Pastor Angelo, who was taking notice of his reply. Pastor Angelo acknowledged Carlos was spiritually led by looking toward heaven then nodding his head in full agreement.

"I want to thank all of you listening tonight, and you too, Cynthia. Very important questions asked and answered. Next week, we will focus more on a specific topic. Ralph will announce on social media outlets with more detail. Keep staying tuned to be informed and involved in what the Church today is doing worldwide. This is The Church podcast. Talk to you next week. Goodbye." Carlos signed off and began to gather his things and rose when Ralph called out to him.

"Carlos, I want you to see something here on my laptop screen." Ralph extended his laptop and placed it closer to Carlos to view. "We had a small audience at the start, slowly increasing through the time of our second question, but when you started addressing the third question, look, after you got hung up on…audience growth spiked to the roof! I'm sure there's going to be chatter about this all over social media. I'll monitor it."

Pastor Angelo came over to see those results and numbers. "Hundreds of thousands, and this is the first podcast!" Pastor Angelo looked at Carlos in amazement.

Carlos looked over at Ralph and pointed out, "Hey, Ralph, we have to work on some phone call protocols for the show." Ralph shook his head in agreement. "Let's break down the equipment and box the soundproofing tiles, then we can call it a day." All hands turned to at the tasks at hand and made short work of it.

As Carlos was driving them home, Ralph was sharing the early chatter on social media. "We are getting listeners from all over the world. I'm reading comments from people in Africa, Canada, Europe, Asia, and South America. Haven't read any from Australia yet, but it's still early. I'll keep you both informed."

Pastor Angelo was still amazed at the numbers and kept saying so. "Carlos, God has opened wide a door for you. You will be able now to witness to the lost worldwide with the attraction God has given your podcast and help support the ministry of the Church throughout the world. Praise God!"

"Pastor, Ralph and I were discussing a couple nights ago how important that every person in combat take their personal role seriously. They must conduct it with consideration for the benefit of all their teammates. We are on the Lord's side, to him be all the glory!" Carlos exclaimed.

The days turned into weeks, and they were all flying by. Meanwhile, Pastor Angelo and Carlos continued to experience growth at their own church, having to add an additional service on Sunday to accommodate the new families seeking the Lord. Also, a Friday night service was begun focusing on the young adults and teens to keep them exposed to the things of God. Carlos and Evelyn had both been staying involved, and their lives kept getting busier as they availed themselves to meet needs.

Chapter 10

Carlos was very happy with the growth and spirit of revival that was taking place at his church. He believed that all actions that got them here was to be continued, like prayer. But he believed other practical actions needed to be maintained too, so he kept asking for volunteers to go with him on Saturdays. He made it a practice to go through the neighborhoods and knock on doors and personally invite families to church and offer prayer with them. Some began to look at Carlos like he was a celebrity because his podcast had continued to grow in audience and was talked about on the local news. They were impressed that he would be walking their street and knock on their door with others. Carlos simply always wanted to show that he was a normal person just like them. When this activity concluded for the day, Carlos got everyone home after providing lunch for them. He got nothing for himself; he stayed in prayer for the people they had met and talked to, remembering their needs and petitioning God's favor upon each of them. Before heading back to the church to meet with Pastor Angelo, Carlos thought it good to go home and check on Evelyn. Evelyn was now a full nine months pregnant.

Pulling into his driveway, Carlos noticed Edna Boyce's car there, so he figured she was there with Eddy-Boy for rehearsal with Evelyn. Just as he thought, when he got inside, he saw Eddy-Boy setting up an electronic keyboard and microphone to a set of speakers. Edna Boyce came walking out his kitchen, having with her a sandwich and beverage. She intended to eat as she watched Eddy-Boy rehearse with Evelyn. When she saw Carlos, she was surprised. "Carlos, we were told that you would be gone all day. Since we now have Friday night service, we moved the rehearsal date to Saturday now. Plus, I wanted to be company for Evelyn. She is about due to have her baby," Edna explained.

"Thanks, Edna," Carlos responded. "I really appreciate that. I was on my way over to the church but thought, 'I should check on Ev.' So here I am. Plus, I wanted to grab a bite to eat. I guess I'll make me a sandwich too."

Edna set down her sandwich and beverage. "I'll make one for you, and I'll bring you a drink too." Edna stepped back toward the kitchen.

As she departed, Carlos turned toward Eddy-Boy and asked, "Where's Evelyn?"

"She went upstairs saying she had something to do. You know she's not moving that fast right now, so I'm setting things up to be ready when she comes back down," Eddy-Boy informed Carlos.

Carlos was looking at Eddy-Boy as he responded and said, "We missed you today when we were doing home visitation in the community. I really enjoy your bold witness for Jesus Christ. It also helps encourage the girls to speak out and not be shy. But even more than that, I like how you always keep it real."

"Thanks, Carlos," Eddy-Boy said as he turned toward Carlos. "Mom asked to come over and practice today because Evelyn told her you would be gone all day. We can plan another day to rehearse if you want us to…"

"No, you're timing today is perfect because I will be gone most of the day. Evelyn can use the company. I'll be leaving in a few minutes." Carlos turned and went and sat down and started reviewing his notes to share with Pastor Angelo for their weekly meeting.

Eddy-Boy followed Carlos and told him, "I been working on a number of songs I think I'm ready to start performing. Maybe I can start on Friday nights at church?"

Just then, Evelyn appeared. Walking toward the electronic keyboard Eddy-Boy set up for her, she approached slowly with a noticeable waddle. "Okay, Eddy-Boy, take a drink of water and let's start rehearsing your scales."

"Sister Evelyn, I already rehearsed them this morning at home when I got up this morning. I wanted to start rehearsing those songs you bought soundtracks to so I'm prepared to start performing them on Friday night now at church. Please, just sit down, relax today, and let me perform for you and Carlos." Eddy-Boy then took Evelyn by the hand and led her to a loveseat to sit and be comfortable on.

Meanwhile, Edna arrived with a sandwich and drink for Carlos and placed it on the coffee table before him. Eddy-Boy went and grabbed his microphone and boom box then returned to his audience. Having popped in a CD containing a musical soundtrack and grabbing the microphone, Eddy-Boy spoke into it. "I couldn't have chosen a better audience for my first audience. Your commitment to Christ and your discipline in living it inspire me to constantly be thankful for the grace shed upon me." Eddy-Boy adjusted his posture as he prepared to sing.

Carlos was still engrossed in his notes and arranging them for presentation later when Evelyn grabbed his attention by shouting, "Carlos!" Then she pointed with her whole arm to direct his attention to the moment. Carlos finally raised his gaze and moved to sit close to Evelyn in the loveseat, then he grabbed his sandwich and drink and began to eat as he watched Eddy-Boy perform.

Eddy-Boy begins singing "Grace (Acoustic)" by Saint James. Evelyn and Carlos both watched and listened with enthusiasm, Evelyn was paying attention to his performance, Carlos was loving the words and music. He kept bopping his head as he continued to enjoy his sandwich. As the song and its melody concluded Carlos and Evelyn were deeply touched by Eddy-Boy and shared their remarks.

"That was a great song, loved it. I saw myself in the words of it!" Carlos emphasized.

Evelyn was pleased and leaned forward and told Eddy-Boy, "That was a genuine heartfelt performance."

Eddy-Boy looked at Evelyn, for he was trying to impress her and said, "I listened and studied the song, how I could make it my own. I know Saint James wrote it, but I wanted to sing it like he wrote it for me to perform and share it."

"That's it! That's what I wanted you to learn. Every performance has to be a real expression of your spirit. I'm proud of you. The discipline of practice will always then show your perfection." Evelyn commented with pride. Carlos finished his sandwich and then washed it down with his drink. Carlos began to pick up his glass and plate to return to the kitchen when Evelyn stopped him by saying, "Leave it!"

"Okay then, I have to get going. Ev, I don't know how long I will be, but I'll be back as soon as our meeting is over. Thank you two for being here. And Edna, thanks for the sandwich, you make a great sandwich. See you all later." Carlos went and gathered all his notes and placed them in his pocket.

Eddy-Boy wanted to continue singing, so he went and got more soundtracks to perform before Evelyn and his mother.

Carlos came back to Evelyn and deeply hugged her and told her, "Don't cook anything tonight, I'll bring dinner home tonight. What do you want?"

"You know what I have a taste for," Evelyn surprised Carlos. "I'd like Hawaiian pizza and rice pudding."

"Okaaay. I will call you when I am on my way and will pick up those items on the way home." Carlos kisses Evelyn and leaves.

Pastor Angelo was already at the church when Carlos arrived. He also had items he wanted to share with Carlos when he got there, so he waited for Carlos in his office. When Carlos came inside his office and was invited to sit, he was all eager to share his reports, so he started pulling out his small stack of notes from his pocket. As he did, Pastor Angelo began to share some comments. "Carlos, these are indeed exciting times. Our church is growing in a variety of ways. We continue to see more and more families now regularly attend our weekly worship services, Friday nights are now full of youth and young adult activity. They are showing a hunger for the Word of God, a lively worship experience, and it's always beautiful to see that the Lord Jesus is the center and joy of all their fellowship. We are truly in the midst of a revival experience."

Carlos was noticing the joy evident in Pastor Angelo's face as he shared his observations. "These are the fruits of your faithful labor, now being harvested. To God be the glory! Let me share some of these that I have on my notes because there is more to give God praise for, for He is worthy! We continue to announce the need for world missions evangelization and Bible translation. However, there are entire countries that are not accepting of anyone entering their country sharing the Gospel, but, should they have communities needing aid or suffering from disaster, God has raised up ministries like 'Samaritan's Purse,' which we call the worldwide audience to support. And the Gospel is still being preached with their very lives in service to their neighbor, praise God!" Carlos began to grab more notes to share in his report.

Pastor Angelo sat up in his chair and pulled closer to his desk to join in the conversation again. "Carlos, this is great and exciting news that you are sharing, but one thing I wanted to do is finally take the time and share with you about—"

As Pastor Angelo was speaking, Carlos' phone began vibrating. Carlos looked at his phone and saw it was from home, he thought it was Evelyn, so he asked Pastor Angelo, "Could you forgive me, Pastor, this is Evelyn calling me." Pastor Angelo nodded in agreement as Carlos turned and stepped away from his chair.

"Hello, Ev, what's going on we're in a meeting right now—" Carlos asked.

The voice was not Evelyn's but Eddy-Boy's. "It's me Eddy-Boy, Mom is taking Evelyn now to the hospital. She's going to have the baby! Meet us there. I got to go." Eddy-Boy hangs up and leaves Carlos in silence.

Carlos turns back toward Pastor Angelo in shock and informs him, "I left Edna and Eddy-Boy at home with Evelyn before I came here. They're taking her to the hospital. She's ready to have the baby." Carlos sat down with a bewildered look on his face.

"Then let's go meet them there. I'll drive, you need to breathe, Carlos. Let's go. We can pick up Sister Maria on the way. She will definitely want to be there." Pastor Angelo took charge of the moment and grabbed Carlos and led him to his car and departed.

After picking up Sister Maria, and she saw the bewildered look on Carlos' face, she turned to him and told him, "You better man up right now and show Evelyn that you are the man. Be strong for her!"

"I've never been through anything like this. I've never felt that kind of pain," Carlos worriedly stated.

"You probably never will, but for her sake, you've got to feel like you're going through it with her and pull her through with confidence and joy. Hopefully, she hasn't delivered yet so you can go through this with her. Are you ready to do this?" Sister Maria gave Carlos the serious eye.

"A-hem…yes." Carlos collected himself and changed his bearing.

Pastor Angelo dropped Sister Maria and Carlos at the door of the hospital before he went to park the car. Sister Maria was familiar with the staff there, so she enquired for Carlos where Evelyn was.

"She's in the LDR[24] now. She already completed her paperwork. Is he the baby's father? She's in labor and dilating quickly. You are right on time. Take him over to her now," the nurse said and moved on.

Carlos came to the room where Evelyn was and saw she was already experiencing intense labor pains. As soon as she saw Carlos,

---

[24] A room designation short for labor-delivery-recovery.

as he approached her, Evelyn stared at him and screamed, "Carlos, help me push this baby out!" with extreme emphasis.

"Her doctor is here and prepping for her delivery. He'll be here any second now. Get comfortable alongside of her," said the labor and delivery nurse.

"Ev, I'm here now. Two are better than one. We'll handle this together. We'll get through this." Carlos kept speaking encouraging words to Evelyn as a show of support.

When the doctor arrived and quickly examined Evelyn, he noticed that her cervix was now fully dilated and ordered, "Prep now for delivery, STAT!" The delivery nurse suddenly began moving quickly and in an orderly way throughout the room making all preparation immediately for Evelyn's delivery. The doctor tried to relax Evelyn by assuring her, "Okay, Evelyn, I've done this plenty of times. I know it hurts, but when I let you know to push, I want you to push real hard. You're really dilated, hopefully this won't take long. Okay?!"

"Yes, Doc," Carlos answered, "we will be doing this together!" Evelyn just nodded her head quickly while taking deep breaths.

The doctor looked up and over at Carlos and responded, "Good man!"

The delivery was brief, despite the labor pain continuing throughout the delivery process. Evelyn gave birth to a son, who was given to the delivery nurse and cleaned up before being placed into the arms of Evelyn. The doctor always admiringly looked upon the parents as they received their newborn child then enquired, "What name have you two decided on for your extremely healthy son?"

Carlos removed his gaze from Evelyn and their son and said, "Angelo, after the man of God, our pastor." The doctor acknowledged the response with a nod.

Just then, Evelyn spoke up and told to the doctor. "His middle name will be Felipé, after the man of God, his grandfather."

"Very well. Nurse, his name is Angelo Felipé." The doctor informs the delivery nurse as she enters the detail in her computer, amongst handling other post-partum details.

Evelyn cradled her newborn son in amazement as she could now kiss young Angelo that she bore for the past nine months. She continued looking over her son, appreciating the wonderful gift of life the Lord had given her and Carlos. She then informed Carlos, "Carlos, I love your father. I never told you this before, but I only had one conversation with your dad, and it was on our wedding day. We spoke briefly, and he was so proud of you." Evelyn turned and looked at Carlos. "He told me, 'My son Carlos will be a great man. You are marrying a great man!' Of course, at the time, I was thinking he was only trying to talk you up to me as a good dad would on his son's wedding day, but knowing now the kind of man he was, and the things in you I've seen accomplished, he spoke with the confidence of God. So we will now never forget him, our son shall carry his name and my prayer today for him will be for him to grow and be like his grandfather with self-sacrificing obedience and living in the confidence of God!"

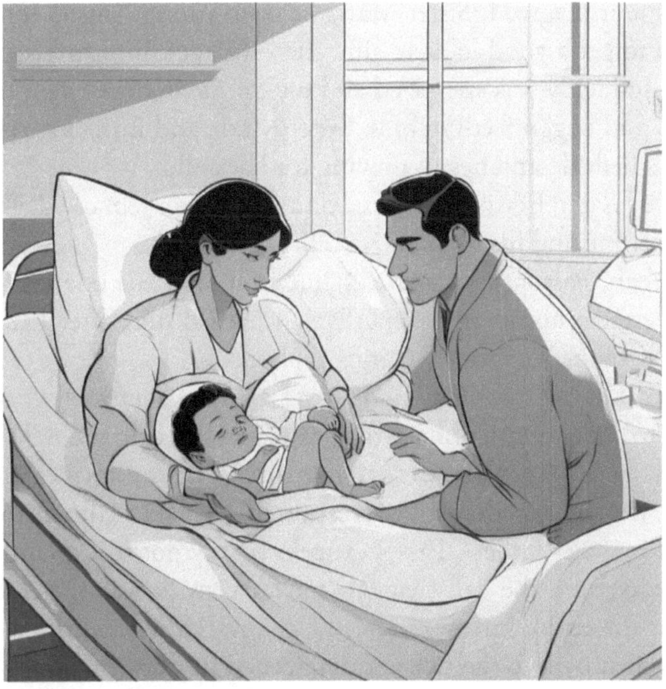

"Great prayer! Our son will need all the prayer he can get, and you and I will be the main ones providing it daily on his behalf. Let me hold him, Evelyn." Carlos was eager to hold Angelo.

"Here, take him and let me get some rest. I can use some sleep right now." Evelyn smiled, seeing the joy on Carlos' face.

"Pastor Angelo and Sister Maria are also here, waiting outside the room. Should I invite them in?" Carlos was cuddling Angelo, all full of pride in his newborn son. The delivery nurse was still present and asked Carlos if he would like her to put young Angelo in a portable incubator while she prepared his first meal. Carlos handed him over to her and went and invited Pastor Angelo, Sister Maria, Edna Boyce, and Eddy-Boy in to see Evelyn and young Angelo. As they entered, Carlos announced to them, "Ev was strong during delivery and let me introduce to you our son, Angelo Felipé DeLeon."

Sister Maria looked adoringly upon young Angelo. The delivery nurse had prepared his first meal in a small bottle, so Sister Maria asked if she could take the child to his mother for his first feeding, and the nurse agreed. Sister Maria held up young Angelo for Pastor Angelo to get a good look at him, then she took him to his mother. Evelyn suddenly was energized and took pride in once again holding Angelo and began feeding him. Sister Maria and Edna sat alongside Evelyn's bedside and began praying for her child.

Carlos and Eddy-Boy looked on as the pastor remarked, "Named him after me and his grandpa, excellent choices!"

"Yeah, Pastor, I wanted to name him after the one man that I highly esteem above all others. Evelyn named him after Dad so he would never be forgotten," Carlos explained.

"You know what Carlos that was along the lines of what I was trying to talk to you about when you got the call about Evelyn. I wanted to fully explain to you that many of the incidents of the revival we are experiencing were prayed for and claimed to come to pass by your father." Pastor Angelo finally got to explain. "Your father answered the call that few men accept, it was the calling to care for the entire kingdom of God as a watchman on the wall. He put his own pain to the side and interceded for the kingdom of God. He never forgot about you, as the results are evident in your life. He put the priorities of God above all else and trusted God to satisfy his need. He loved you, Carlos, and if he couldn't have a relationship with you, your earthly Father, he wanted you to have one then with your Heavenly Father. Now, today you have become a father, now you can truly understand the weight that position carries. But remember, God still stays number one, remember your father."

Carlos was taking in the words of Pastor Angelo deep into his heart so he would never forget. "My dad was successful. He lived up to the standard God called him to be."

"We all miss him, Carlos," Pastor Angelo acknowledged. "I wish I had more men like him! Thank God he prayed and asked God to give me you, a young man of God!"

"Pastor, there is something I need to do after you bring me back to pick up my car from the church," Carlos realized.

Sister Edna overheard Carlos and jumped into their conversation, "Pastor, if you're going to take him to get his car, I can bring Sister Maria home when we are done here and Evelyn is resting."

"I appreciate that, Edna, you're saving me a trip. Maria, I'll see you back at home." Pastor then turned and looked at Carlos and says, "Okay, Carlos, what do you have to do? I'll take you now."

Carlos looked at Evelyn feeding young Angelo and said, "Evelyn, I'll be back as soon as I'm done. Pastor, the something I need to do I should have done a long time ago, I need to go back to the cemetery and honor my father."

Epilogue

Pastor Angelo and Carlos departed from the hospital, and Eddy-Boy tagged along. He was tired of being around the hospital already, plus, he was hungry. Eddy-Boy was enjoying the idea of being able to hang out with the two men of God at his Church, so he took fun in joining in with Pastor Angelo in reminding Carlos of his new responsibilities such as diaper changing, feeding, lack of sleep, and the whole change in lifestyle. As they arrived at the church and pulled alongside Carlos' car, Pastor Angelo asked Carlos, "Carlos, I'm sorry. I never asked you earlier if you wanted me to go with you to the cemetery. We can go together right now."

"No, thank you for asking. I'll be all right," Carlos assured Pastor Angelo. "I have some personal acknowledgments to share, many thanksgivings, and a recommitment of my life and ministry. Afterward, I have to get back to Evelyn and Angelo. Also, I have to let Mom know and pick her up and bring her over."

"Don't worry about your mother. I'll make sure she gets there," Pastor Angelo informed Carlos. He looked at Eddy-Boy in the backseat and told him, "C'mon, get up here in front. We can go get something to eat." Carlos exited the car, and Eddy-Boy rushed to the front seat. As he did, Pastor Angelo turned on his radio, which was tuned onto K-Love Radio starting a new song by Ty Brasel, "God Is the Best" with 1K Phew.

"Yeah, turn that up! I love that song!" Eddy-Boy swayed and bobbed as he listened.

"Ohhh, to be young again. I'll see you later, Carlos." Pastor Angelo shook his head as he turned up the volume and slowly pulled away.

Carlos watched as they left; he was enjoying the song too. When they were gone, he looked at his car, then he looked up at the Church, then he looked around at where he was at and looked up and said,

"Thank you, Father!" Carlos stepped to his car and took his seat and started his car; he let it run for a while as he thought of the day's events and where he was now going. When he was ready, he engaged his gear shifter and departed for the cemetery.

As Carlos approached the cemetery, he slowed down thinking about the Scripture: "It is appointed for man, to die once and after this comes judgment."[25] He arrived at the section where he had his father buried and pulled his car curbside and got out. Carlos walked up to the gravesite and stood, looking at the humble headstone of his father. He remembered his attitude and thoughts of his father when he was last here. Carlos lowered his head in humility, realizing he was very wrong about his father. He straightened up and began to speak, "Heavenly Father, I thank you for my dad. I am a very fortunate man

to have been loved and raised by him. I realize that it was all my fault that we had no relationship as I became an adult and started making my own decisions. This is something I will have to forgive myself for and then forget about it. But God, there is nothing impossible with you. The last time I was here, we laid my father's body to rest. I had little regard for him, for I thought that I was the successful one, and he wasn't. Now, I know it's the other way around. He kept you first over everything else. I am here now to honor him. I pray that my dad, Juan Felipé, knows that his life was not in vain, and that his many prayers are still being answered. I want to address him now as I speak…

"Dad, today I have become a father too. Evelyn and I have a son. I named him Angelo after the pastor, but Evelyn named him Felipé so we will never forget you. I now understand the weight and gravity of being a father, I believe I understand you a lot more now.

---

[25] Hebrews 9:27

I've accepted the call to ministry and am Pastor Angelo's associate pastor. What helped me mostly was that study Bible you bought for me. Since the day I got it, I have been faithful in keeping my word to read it every day. It has comforted and encouraged me through life, but even more than that, it has helped me to see and know our eternal God. Ever since I first learned that you were a man of prayer, I've taken it upon myself to follow in your footsteps. It has certainly helped me to intimately know God as our Father, but I also learned to be entirely dependent upon Him and not anything or anyone else. I know you had been praying for revival long before I started, but it is great to report to you God is sending the latter rains. Revival is here, and it's just starting! Our church is growing with people. Individuals and whole families are answering the call from God to repent and prepare for his return. God is honoring every obedient effort we put forth. We are making use of social media to share the Gospel but have also developed a worldwide audience with our weekly podcast. There we keep promoting worldwide missionary work and Bible translation needs, but we also have opened a door for all churches to network with each other to share information, available services, and needs. Dad, I am committed to the work of ministry for the Lord Jesus Christ. I want you to know your prayers for the church, and for your son were never in vain. I miss you, Dad!" Carlos took a moment to vent his emotion, and then he concluded by saying, "But like Mom reminded me, we will see you again." Carlos stood, looking down upon the gravesite, then lifting his gaze forward, he realized that all things had worked together for good.[26] Before turning and leaving, Carlos looked up toward heaven and slowly uttered, "Thank you!"

When Carlos got back to his car, he sped off to quickly get back to the hospital. As he was driving, he constantly was reminding himself that he was a dad now. As he arrived, the nurses immediately recognized Carlos as he entered and one of them escorted him to the LDR where Evelyn was staying. When he entered the room, Evelyn was resting in her bed, and his mama, Lucita was holding her grandson Angelo. She was pacing the floor praying and singing songs to

---

[26] Romans 8:28

him. Carlos went alongside Evelyn's bed and sat and clutched her hand. She awoke and looked at Carlos and smiled lovingly at him just as Lucita brought Angelo before them, who also was all smiles.

Carlos slowly shook his head and declared, "This day is full of new beginnings!"

End.

Praise! To His Eternal Holiness!

To the Church of God: A song by Alfredo

(Intro) Praise… Praise… Praise… Praise…

(Chorus) Praise! To His Eternal Holiness! (Repeat 4×)

1. All flesh is as grass
   Withering and blown away,
   But His Word stands sure
   Forever and every day!
   (Chorus)

2. You see, God has a way
   To make bones live again.
   This is done for the man
   Who puts his faith in Him!
   (Repeat chorus)

3. Our adversary Satan
   Distracts and entices
   But keep looking unto Jesus
   He exposed his devices
   (Chorus)

4. The day will come
   When we're gathered before
      the Lord
   With one voice we'll sing
   To the one that we adore!

(Repeat chorus twice)

(Final Chorus, sung 4×, rising pitch)
Praise! Praise! Praise! Praise! Praise! Praise! Praise!
To His eternal holiness! To His eternal holiness!

About the Author

Alfredo Santos Metoyer is a native-born Chicagoan. Writing, for him, was always a secret ambition ever since he was a seven-year-old boy begging his mother to buy him a copy of Edgar Rice Burroughs *Tarzan of the Apes*. He wept and was amazed at the author's ability to affect his thoughts, emotions, and feelings by telling that story. Having accepted Jesus Christ as his personal Savior and Lord at the age of fifteen, he poured his life into knowing him by daily reading Scripture and selfless service. He claims writing is now his service within the body of Christ. He has two adult children and two granddaughters, all living near him in Aurora, Illinois.

www.ingramcontent.com/pod-product-compliance
Lightning Source LLC
Chambersburg PA
CBHW062226150726

47991CB00006B/2453